About ISTE

The International Society for Technology in Education (ISTE) is the trusted source for professional development, knowledge generation, advocacy, and leadership for innovation. A nonprofit membership association, ISTE provides leadership and service to improve teaching, learning, and school leadership by advancing the effective use of technology in PK–12 and teacher education.

Home of the National Educational Technology Standards (NETS), the Center for Applied Research in Educational Technology (CARET), and ISTE's annual conference (formerly known as the National Educational Computing Conference, or NECC), ISTE represents more than 100,000 professionals worldwide. We support our members with information, networking opportunities, and guidance as they face the challenge of transforming education. To find out more about these and other ISTE initiatives, visit our website at **www.iste.org**.

As part of our mission, ISTE Book Publishing works with experienced educators to develop and produce practical resources for classroom teachers, teacher educators, and technology leaders. Every manuscript we select for publication is carefully peer-reviewed and professionally edited. We value your feedback on this book and other ISTE products. E-mail us at **books@iste.org**.

About the Authors

Camille Cole

A former high school social studies and technology applications teacher, Nancy "Camille" Cole has worked in the educational technology field for more than 20 years and has been an educator for 30 years. Camille is a graduate of the University of Oregon's School of Education, in Eugene, Oregon, and has participated in graduate studies in educational technology and education policy and administration at both the University of Oregon and Portland State University, in Portland, Oregon. From 1998 to 2006, as part of a partnership between the Oregon Association of Education Service Districts and the Oregon Department of Education, she oversaw the deployment and implementation of the Oregon Access Network, a statewide interactive videoconferencing (IVC) network. She is currently the principal of Schoolhouse Communications, a virtual learning consulting firm. You can reach her at schoolhouse2@comcast.net.

Camille has served on Oregon's K–12 Distance Education Council, the Oregon Telecommunications Coordinating Council, Oregon Online Leaders advisory group, Portland State University's Preparing Tomorrow's Teachers to Use Technology advisory board, and as chair of the Oregon Lewis & Clark Distance Education Showcase Steering Committee. She is a member in good standing of the North American Council for Online Learning. Camille also works as a freelance fiction writer. Her short stories have been published in several literary journals. She is currently working on a novel.

Kecia Ray

Kecia Campbell-Ray began her career as a middle school science teacher in Dekalb County, Georgia. She taught in one of the first 21st-Century classrooms in the state of Tennessee. Dr. Ray conducted research in technology literacy assessment as an Assistant Professor at Middle Tennessee State University before being invited to develop the technology design for Frist Center for the Visual Arts. In 2000, she became the Director of Technology Research in the Office of Science Outreach at Vanderbilt University School of Medicine.

Dr. Ray is a member of the International Society for Technology in Education (ISTE) where she is the elected Vice President of the Telecom Special Interest Group. She is an invited member of the North American Council for Online Learning Research Committee and an invited Commissioner with the Montessori Accreditation Council for Teacher Education. She has conducted research in the area of technology integration across the U.S., and in Canada and South Africa. She is an

Videoconferencing
for K–12 Classrooms

Second Edition

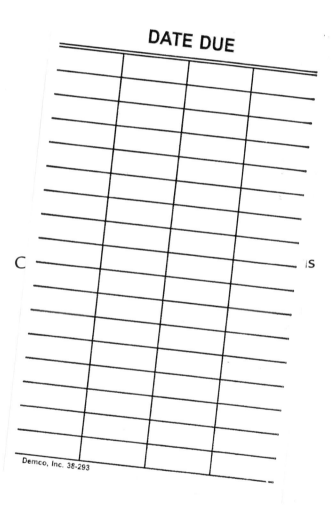

DATE DUE

C ——————————————————— is

Demco, Inc. 38-293

International Society for Technology in Education
EUGENE, OREGON • WASHINGTON, DC

Videoconferencing for K–12 Classrooms, *Second Edition*
A Program Development Guide

Camille Cole • Kecia Ray • Jan Zanetis

© 2009 International Society for Technology in Education

Director of Book Publishing: *Courtney Burkholder*
Acquisitions Editor: *Jeff V. Bolkan*
Production Editors: *Lynda Gansel, Lanier Brandau*
Production Coordinator: *Rachel Bannister*
Graphic Designer and Cover Design: *Signe Landin*
Copy Editor: *Nancy Olson*
Book Design and Production: *Kim McGovern*

Library of Congress Cataloging-in-Publication Data

Cole, Camille.
  Videoconferencing for K-12 classrooms: a program development guide /
Camille Cole, Kecia Ray, Jan Zanetis. — 2nd ed.
      p. cm.
  Includes bibliographical references.
  ISBN 978-1-56484-256-5 (pbk.)
  1. Teleconferencing in education. 2. Videoconferencing. I. Ray, Kecia.
II. Zanetis, Jan. III. Title.
  LB1044.9.T38C65 2009
  371.3'58—dc22

                                                    2009005035

Second Edition
ISBN: 978-1-56484-256-5

Printed in the United States of America

International Society for Technology in Education (ISTE)
Washington, DC, Office:
      1710 Rhode Island Ave. NW, Suite 900, Washington, DC 20036-3132
Eugene, Oregon, Office:
      180 West 8th Ave., Suite 300, Eugene, OR 97401-2916
Order Desk: 1.800.336.5191
Order Fax: 1.541.302.3778
Customer Service: orders@iste.org
Book Publishing: books@iste.org
Book Sales and Marketing: booksmarketing@iste.org
Rights and Permissions: permissions@iste.org
Web: www.iste.org

author of books and articles focused on teaching through technology and consults with school systems, universities, and museums designing learning networks. Dr. Ray presents nationally and internationally and serves as adjunct professor in the College of Natural and Applied Sciences at Lipscomb University as well as graduate faculty for the college of Teaching and Learning at University of Maryland University College. She currently serves as the Assistant Superintendent of Federal Programs and Grants for Metropolitan Nashville Public Schools, Tennessee, where she oversees district policy and planning, administration of federal and categorical grants, family and community engagement, and professional development. She resides in Nashville with her husband, Dr. Clark Ray.

Jan Zanetis

Jan Zanetis is a career educator with 20 plus years in the K–12 classroom. Currently she is the Market Manager for Education at TANDBERG, the global leader in videoconferencing solutions. She came to TANDBERG from Vanderbilt University where she served as the Director of the Virtual School. At the Virtual School she developed hundreds of hours of interactive video lessons for K–12 classrooms featuring Vanderbilt faculty as presenters. The Virtual School became a leading distance learning provider during her directorship.

Jan is well known for presenting professional development sessions for educators and has keynoted various education technology conferences. She has co-written two ISTE books and has contributed several articles in various education journals. Jan currently serves on the board of directors of the U.S. Distance Learning Association and is the president emeritus of the special interest group within ISTE, SIGIVC. Jan lives in Nashville, Tennessee with her husband, Alex and is the proud mom of three sons.

Acknowledgments

We would like to thank all of the teachers, content developers, and school administrators who shared their videoconferencing stories with us. Their real-life stories put a face on this book that will help everyone understand the potential of this technology in the classroom.

We would also like to thank our families for their support and encouragement during the writing of this book.

Contents

Chapter 4

Planning a Videoconference 63

Preface

Videoconferencing for K–12 Classrooms, Second Edition is for teachers and instructional technology coordinators who are looking for ways to use interactive videoconferencing (IVC) in the classroom to help students meet and exceed today's rigorous educational standards. We have outlined the benefits IVC can provide in an educational setting, provided an overview of how the technology works and how much it might cost, and presented a planning list of necessary equipment. We have also provided step-by-step directions for integrating IVC into the curriculum and detailed examples of how this technology is currently being employed to achieve core curriculum standards. In addition, you will find numerous vignettes scattered throughout the book chronicling real-life classrooms throughout the world where teachers and students are engaged in educational exchanges via interactive videoconferencing.

A glossary of key terms is provided in Appendix C; words defined in the glossary will appear in bold italics when first used in the text.

Introduction

The Virtual Education Explosion

Increasing access to emerging communications technologies has provided, or will soon provide, K–12 classrooms throughout the world with the ability to take advantage of educational resources, cultural partnerships, and expert mentoring once available only to those in close proximity to large research universities and major urban areas. You've heard this teaching or delivery method referred to as *virtual classrooms,* cyber schools, online education, web-based instruction, *interactive videoconferencing (IVC)*, e-learning, distance learning, *distributed learning,* and so forth. For the purpose of this book on interactive videoconferencing for the K–12 classroom, we will refer to the overall contemporary *distance education* movement as *virtual learning.* IVC is one of many emerging virtual learning *modalities.* Our plan is to demonstrate to you, as a K–12 classroom teacher, what videoconferencing is, how you and your students can benefit from this powerful technology, and what you need to know to make the most effective use of it in your classroom today.

To fully appreciate what IVC can do for us today that we have never been able to do before, it's helpful to take a quick look at the history of distance education in the United States and the rapid rise of virtual learning in K–12 schools since the start of the 21st century. Distance education has been around a lot longer than many of the educational technologies that we take for granted today—certainly longer than the personal computer. Distance education, in its broadest sense, is the separation of teacher and learner through time or space, or both.

A Brief History

Distance education has been around since the first teacher mailed the first correspondence course to a remote student centuries ago. Who knows, perhaps even Socrates sent an essay to Plato asking him to ponder it and respond via messenger. Over time, as communication technologies have become more available, convenient, and instantaneous, distance education programs have incorporated ever more advanced modes of content delivery: radio, television, audiotapes, and interactive computer programs. The current generation of technology-based distance learning programs is the product of centuries of experience and development in distance education.

Over the last quarter century, virtual learning has undergone tremendous changes as delivery options have metamorphosed and the number of students interested and able to tap its potential has exploded. Universities were the first to jump on the virtual learning bandwagon. University correspondence courses were made available to military personnel, citizens living abroad, and people physically unable to attend classes for any reason. Over time, these courses have evolved to include audiotapes, videotapes, TV cable and satellite broadcasts, desktop microcomputers, the *Internet,* and IVC technologies. While the first 20 years of growth was primarily in postsecondary applications, K–12 education has increasingly taken to virtual learning in the last few years, a trend that is likely to drive the next evolutionary cycle in instructional delivery methods. Thanks to technological advances and funding opportunities such as *E-rate,* K–12 educators have joined the growing number of *virtual teachers* and *virtual students* worldwide.

Following is a brief history of the key developmental breakthroughs that have made possible interactive videoconferencing for education:

In 1956, AT&T developed the original picture phone test system. This was the first time voice and video were delivered simultaneously over a single phone line. The interest in developing this technology was driven by Cold War fears and the desire to develop advanced technologies for gathering intelligence, in which *telecommunications* would play a pivotal role.

In 1969, Department of Defense officials began transmitting voice over the ARPANet (Advanced Research Projects Agency Network), the precursor to the Internet.

In 1981, the Annenberg Corporation began the development of television courses, and Public Broadcasting launched the Adult Learning Service. At the same time, colleges and universities began offering satellite courses, many of which became online courses as the Internet became more accessible to the general public. K–12 schools did not generally have access to these technology resources in the early 1980s, but K–12 classroom teachers were beginning to learn how to utilize desktop computers as a teaching and administrative tool, which eventually led to the integration of Internet resources, software applications, and data collection tools into the K–12 environment.

By 1992, electronic conferences were regularly taking place through the use of interactive videoconferencing technology. One example from this period was the Global Electronic Shakespeare Conference held in 1992, where professors, journalists, and dignitaries debated Shakespearean literature and new archival discoveries. This was also the year that K–12 teachers were first introduced to the potential of videoconferencing in the classroom, in the form of an *application* called CUseeME, developed by Tim Dorcey of Cornell University. The camera most frequently used in classrooms for CUseeMe resembled an eyeball and sat on top of the computer monitor. The camera (with a built-in microphone) was connected to the computer and used the computer's *modem* to transmit voice and video via the Internet through a *56K* connection over a regular phone line (or a 128K *ISDN* [Integrated Services Digital Network] digital phone line connection). CUseeMe was relatively easy to use and allowed teachers and students sitting in front of a computer to talk with and see someone located hundreds or thousands of miles away.

The 1990s were a time of K–12 teachers' growing awareness of computer technologies in the classroom, including e-mail, the **World Wide Web,** and multimedia software. In 1997 a massive effort was launched across the United States to wire schools and purchase computer equipment. Often, this was a true grassroots effort, with parents stringing cable through school buildings and community groups providing needed hardware and software. Eventually, the folks in Washington, D.C., took note and established the E-rate program, offsetting the costs of "getting connected." In 1994, 35% of all public schools in the United States reported having Internet access. By 2000 that figure had climbed to 98% (U.S. Department of Education, 2001). More K–12 teachers began to take advantage of the tremendous resources available on the Internet, reaching across time and space to interact with each other and experts in their field through e-mail, e-mail lists, and online chat rooms. Before long, school buildings and even classrooms had their own web pages. A school's geographical location, the number of books in its library, and the educational software it had managed to acquire were no longer limits to learning for students or teachers.

Educational Videoconferencing

Over the last few years, videoconferencing technology has been adopted by more and more school systems across the country. Districts have set up distance education class-rooms featuring large TV monitors and videoconference **codecs,** making it possible for large classes to be taught by teachers located at other schools and giving students access to courses not offered in their own schools.

As more and more schools have adopted videoconferencing technologies, school networks have become overburdened, and **bandwidth** (or the lack thereof) has become a crucial issue. The increase in bandwidth offered by **T-1,** T-3, and fiber optic connections can support a much clearer image and real-time **synchronous communication,** but these expensive solutions are not yet feasible for many schools. Fortunately, there is now a much faster alternative to ISDN and the standard Internet: Internet2, a network **infrastructure** reserved solely for education and research purposes. Internet2 is not congested by commercial traffic and is therefore perfectly suited for the high-speed connectivity required by educational videoconference users. We will have more to say about Internet2 in Chapter 6.

Another connectivity solution put in place by several states has been the deployment of statewide video networks that allow school districts to share resources and information through videoconferences. Colleges, universities, museums, and science centers also participate in these statewide video networks. Satellite networks, Internet Data Library Systems (IDLS), and interactive television studios are necessary tools for **distance delivery** of courses. Satellite enables colleges to broadcast courses while the class is in progress. Interactive television studios allow for synchronous communication, making it possible for students at **far-sites** to interact with students attending class in the presence of the professor. Interactive television may be taped and rebroadcast either through satellite or through cable. Internet Data Library Systems provide valuable library resources to students attending classes at a distance. Typically, these resources are accessible through a secure connection, in which a user name or password allows students access to e-books, e-journals, and a variety of scanned documents.

Since the middle of the 1990s, the adoption of virtual learning programs in public, private, and charter K–12 schools has made headlines and influenced educators, lawmakers, journalists, parents, interested onlookers, and a new breed of community partners. Experts in the field predict that virtual learning programs will soon reach tens of millions of students on a regular basis (McMahon, 1998).

IVC's Role in Improving Student Performance

While videoconferencing technology has experienced tremendous growth and development over the past decade, research into its impact on student performance has lagged far behind. Given the current emphasis on educational standards and accountability, it is fair to ask how—and how much—IVC technology will help K–12 students achieve core curriculum goals. While it is clear that IVC can supply experiences and opportunities that students would not otherwise have access to in their own classroom or community, can it really help them to succeed as learners?

Though there is, to date, only a limited amount of research on the relationship between the use of IVC technology in K–12 classrooms and student performance, most *early adopters* agree that videoconferencing success should be measured first and foremost by the number and quality of learning opportunities that it provides students, rather than solely by student performance levels. The research that does exist, however, indicates that students who have the opportunity to augment their curriculum with videoconferencing experiences have a greater motivation to learn, and an increased ability to communicate about, the concepts and skills they are accessing (Ward Melville Heritage Organization, 2002, March; Kober, 1990). Similarly, a white paper published by United Nations Educational, Scientific and Cultural Organizations (UNESCO, 2002) indicates that "distance learning, in its various forms, can work and, if well designed, can be educationally legitimate" (p. 17). The paper also notes the limited research in student performance related to distance education and emphasizes the need for funding such research. Other research suggests that utilizing videoconference technology as an instructional tool can be especially beneficial when students are struggling and need one-on-one instruction.

IVC research has, up to now, concentrated on its impact on higher education, where distance-learning technologies have been in place since the 1970s. Moore (1991) points out that distance education not only separates teachers from students but also modifies their roles. Heath (1997) notes that the instructional design process must be particularly well thought out when planning IVC instruction. Berge and Mrozowski (2001), in a summary of research from 1990 to 1999 related to distance education, conclude that student performance does not suffer from the distance mode of delivery. The majority of this research seems to indicate that student performance is primarily a result of good teaching, and good teaching is not substantially affected by the delivery method (Sullivan, Jolly, Foster, & Tompkins, 1994).

Hanor and Hayden (2003) are two researchers who have been studying and modeling the integration of videoconferencing in K–12 for several years. ILAST, a grant-funded program under the direction of Dr. Hanor, is a partnership of California State

University–San Marcos, the San Diego County Office of Education, the North County Professional Development Federation, CTAP Region IX, the San Diego CUE affiliate, and 24 school districts. It offers a 120-hour professional development program targeting the effective use of technology for teaching and learning. Videoconference technology is an integral part of this program, which includes sessions that deal with the integration of videoconferencing technology and instructional strategies. ILAST also utilizes videoconference technology as a delivery tool, allowing the program to reach its many constituents while reducing travel time.

In 2003 Regional Technology in Education Consortiums held a K–12 symposium involving nationally recognized IVC experts. These experts concluded that policy changes should be made and best practices identified in order for IVC in K–12 to be successful. They established guidelines for change in several categories, including goals and audiences, content, professional development, assessment, research, planning for facilities and networks, and funding. The symposium participants agreed that IVC technology should never be the focus of instruction, but only a tool for delivery: it should enhance and enrich the lesson, but it should never be a substitution for the lesson. Teaching teachers to embrace this technology and incorporate it into their curriculum requires that appropriate content be identified and adequate staff development provided. Participants also agreed that increased bandwidth and advances in telecommunications will encourage the use of interactive videoconferencing in K–12 schools, and trailblazing teachers stand ready for the technology to catch up (Holznagel, 2003).

The Future of Educational Videoconferencing

We are certain that virtual learning options for K–12 schools are here to stay. Not only is a paradigm shift occurring in K–12 school districts, a growing movement toward virtual learning opportunities is occurring outside the public classroom as well. Virtual schools are popping up around the nation and around the world, and educators and parents are taking note. Virtual schools have become one of the fastest growing educational movements of the early 21st century. Virtual schools offer courses through the Internet or other web-based modalities. Virtual schools have been chartered by states, developed by universities, and formed by private companies to serve a growing educational marketplace. Many, if not most, students today have the option of taking at least one online or IVC course before they graduate from high school.

Why are educators and students clamoring to take advantage of these technologies and the opportunities they can provide? Numerous reasons can be cited:

- Increased access to educational resources
- Flexibility for the learner
- Equity in opportunities for both teachers and students
- Valuable interchange with the outside world

A report issued by the U.S. Department of Education (2003) says enrollment in virtual learning programs has doubled in the last five years. Why this explosion of popularity? We would argue that, given the ever-increasing pressure of competition from the global economy, the demand for world-class education and higher student performance has skyrocketed and will continue to do so. World-class resources and highly qualified teachers in every subject are simply not available in every city, town, school district, or classroom. Students and teachers must reach beyond these physical borders to virtual centers of learning and information exchange.

Students who have come to be known as **millenials** have taken to these new ways of learning like fish to water. Of course, integration of these new distance technologies into existing institutional frameworks and systems is not always easy sailing; obstacles and inherent frustrations need to be overcome. Over the course of this book, we will identify some of these potential barriers and help you find ways to surmount them so that you and your students will be able to experience the numerous benefits of videoconferencing in the classroom.

A FIRST EXPERIENCE WITH TELECONFERENCING

Charles Kuralt, Television Journalist
From his 1990 memoir **A Life on the Road**

I'll always be glad I met Archibald MacLeish. I was knocked out by his poems in college. Soon after the new satellite made it possible, I moderated a transatlantic television discussion in which MacLeish took part from New York, as did Prime Minister Harold Wilson from London. The picture was one-way only. I said, "Excuse me, Prime Minister..." On the screen, MacLeish and I could see him look up at the camera. "Before we begin," I said, "I would like to introduce Mr. Archibald MacLeish."

"Indeed, indeed," Wilson said, "I am very glad to meet you, Mr. MacLeish!" As he spoke, the Prime Minister of Great Britain stood up to acknowledge the blind introduction of a man who was thousands of miles away. Seeing this, MacLeish also stood. And I, feeling awkward but not knowing what else to do, stood up too.

"I very much admire your poems," Wilson said, and started saying one of them: "A poem should be palpable and mute...as a globed fruit..." When he finished quoting "Ars Poetica" to its author, the Prime Minister sat down and presently the program began. When we were off the air, MacLeish said to me, "Wasn't that the damndest thing, Wilson standing up like that? ...To him it was as if we were all in the same room."

"Brushes with the Famous," from A Life on the Road *by Charles Kuralt, ©1990 by Charles Kuralt. Used by permission of G.P. Putnam's Sons, a division of Penguin Group (USA) Inc.*

Why We Wrote This Book

We believe that interactive videoconferencing has always enabled, and will continue to enable, this kind of profound and very human response in learners and teachers throughout the globe, from the African jungle to the asphalt jungle. As classroom teachers and teacher educators, we have been occupied with deploying, implementing, designing, preparing, utilizing, and administrating telecommunications technology in the classroom for a combined 32 years. We believe in the value of face-to-face instruction and the here-and-now collaboration made possible by videoconferencing. We wrote this book to share our enthusiasm and knowledge with fellow classroom teachers.

Chapter 1

Equipment and Networks

Basic Equipment and Costs

You may already have interactive videoconferencing equipment installed in your school or somewhere in your district. You may even be using IVC regularly. Or, you may have seen it and wondered what it is and why it's there. If so, you are not alone. Many educators who have heard about the technology, or have seen the equipment sitting in a corner in the district office, have no idea what it can do and how it can be used in the classroom to support standards-based curricula. That's why we're here. Read on!

In this book we'll focus primarily on room-sized videoconferencing units, suitable for classes and workshops of 20 people or more. We won't feature any particular make, model, brand name, or **vendor.** Numerous videoconferencing manufacturers and providers serve the K–12 market, and we have no complaints about any of them. Some of the products on the market offer a more affordable solution for the K–12 market than others do; some offer more flexible instructional solutions. We'll outline a range of mid- to high-end IVC tools in the pages that follow.

To begin with, let's outline some of the standard features available in typical room-sized interactive videoconference models.

Standard classroom IVC systems typically include:

- Codec
- Presentation computer
- Document camera
- Microphones
- Mobile cabinets/Carts
- Display devices
- Remote control
- Student camera

Codec

The codec is essentially a signal coder/decoder. This is a key element of the IVC system and serves a function very similar to the modem in your desktop computer. It converts **analog signals** into **digital signals** and vice versa.

Presentation Computer

Many IVC systems are capable of sending "duo-video," which means you can add another source to the signal you are sending from your codec. Simply put, you can show your document camera view, or your computer view, or even a DVD view along with what you are showing with your main camera. **End users** are able to share documents, view PowerPoint presentations, and visit websites while still seeing and hearing the far-site instructor.

Document Camera

Like the traditional overhead projector, the document camera quickly becomes part of your can't-live-without-it teacher tool bag. The document camera is a secondary system camera, capturing images from a front-lit or back-lit platform. You can use the document camera to transmit pictures of paper documents, objects of all kinds, and transparencies. It zooms in or out, adjusts focus, and displays images with uncanny clarity. This camera can also be turned toward the room, acting as a back-up camera. *Note:* if you're using your system for accessing and viewing supplementary content only and don't plan to display anything from your end of the IVC connection, this item can be trimmed from your must-have budget.

An alternative and less expensive option is a flex cam. Though not as effective for viewing documents, it costs much less than a standard document camera and during a videoconference is great at incorporating close-ups of three-dimensional objects. It can be used to view pictures and documents and can even be attached to a microscope. Like the document camera, it can be used as an extra camera, providing an additional camera feed.

This flex cam serves as an economical replacement for the document camera.

Microphones

Videoconferencing systems feature two-way pictures and two-way sound. IVC systems are sound activated by default, and the audio portion of the system controls the video camera. Most offer a variety of on/off options and are activated by the push of a button. This is called "push to talk," and it is very important for students to realize the importance of muting and unmuting microphones if this is the type of mic you have. A light on the top of the microphone indicates if the microphone is on or off. Microphones are connected with wires to the videoconferencing system and sit on tables in front of the students. If your room has multiple microphones, each should be numbered and coordinated with the student camera so that when the student pushes the microphone button, the camera will point in the student's direction at a distance and angle determined by ***preconfigured settings*** for that seating position. Microphone pre-sets can be configured with the remote control; we suggest that you follow the manufacturer's guidelines for microphone setup. Many distance learning classes have ceiling mounted microphones that capture all audio within a 100-ft. circumference and have state of the art echo-canceling features. This is the best audio solution for a permanent IVC location.

Don't cut corners on your audio system. Experienced videoconferencers agree that if the video portion of the conference goes south, you can still continue with the audio portion, but not the other way around.

Mobile Cabinets/Carts

The furniture that the unit sits on serves two primary purposes: one is to provide locked cabinetry for securing IVC equipment, and the second is to provide a certain amount of mobility for the IVC unit. Standard room-sized units generally come with two locking cabinets equipped with solid ball-bearing wheels. Though the wheels give you some mobility, we don't suggest moving a room-sized unit regularly from classroom to classroom; it's best to keep it in one location. When you do need to move it short distances, however, it's critical to have a set of wheels to assist in this maneuver. There may be an occasion to have a one-time IVC event in the gym, auditorium, or media center (if the connectivity is available), and wheeled carts will help make this possible.

Display Devices

The typical classroom setup uses two television monitors. If you'll be using the system for receive-only "banner" projects and programs, you would be able to use one monitor, using a *picture-in-picture (PIP)* program to view the other site (or your site) on the single screen. A major drawback of a one-monitor system is that when you want to present multimedia materials, it is very helpful to be able to monitor your presentation as well as the reaction at the other end.

Other display options include LCD projectors and electronic whiteboards. An LCD projector or whiteboard can be easily used as a display device for the IVC unit and is particularly useful when you have a large audience. Many of today's classrooms already have one of these devices installed, which could save you money when considering the purchase of displays for your videoconference unit. The downside of these options is that as you "stretch" the video image, you lose a bit of sharpness. Also, dimming the lights for a better image reduces the far-site's ability to view the audience.

Two monitors enable you to present multimedia materials and view the audience at the same time.

With picture-in-picture, students in three remote sites across the United States participate in a writing videoconference with Professor Susan Ford Wiltshire of Vanderbilt University.

Remote Control

This infrared control tool can do more than your TV remote control at home. It drives the camera, allowing you to zoom in and out and side to side. It can also operate an array of special functions available on your particular IVC system. To be successful with IVC, it's a good idea to spend plenty of time learning how to operate the remote control.

A typical remote control.

Student Camera

This is a small camera that generally sits atop a monitor located in front of the classroom. It captures the image of the on-site audience, which may be students, a group of teachers, workshop participants, and so forth. It pans, tilts, and zooms as directed by the microphones or the remote control unit. If only one student camera is available (i.e., no teacher camera set up in the back of the room), the teacher or presenter (if located on-site) must sit with the on-site audience and face the monitor(s) and student camera. (We'll tell you about the teacher camera option in the next section.)

Phone/Fax

It's a good idea to have a phone and a fax connected to an outside line in your virtual classroom. This facilitates direct communication with other sites in case of problems with the IVC system or connection.

These pieces of equipment are basic to almost any classroom interactive videoconference system. Once deployed, this system allows you to see and hear people at one or more remote IVC sites. It also facilitates further interaction through document sharing and shared Internet access. Computers, phone, and fax provide additional communication options.

Estimated start-up costs for this basic classroom system, based on today's market values and including all the features listed above (excluding the phone/fax and computer), range from $5,000 to $30,000. Clearly, there are many choices available, depending on your school's or district's budget. We suggest shopping on vendor websites to get a better idea of what is currently being offered at your particular price point.

Peripherals and Bells and Whistles

The list of equipment above includes all the basics required to carry out successful two-way interactive videoconferencing via a room-sized system, allowing participants to see and hear each other, send and receive video and audio, manipulate system functions, and display information, objects, and media presentations.

In addition to the basics, numerous add-ons can extend your IVC system's capabilities and make it easier to use, especially if you want to present comprehensive class work or workshops that will require you to switch often from camera to camera and from one type of media to another.

Following is a list and brief description of what we believe are key items to consider when expanding or fine-tuning a videoconference system. These are the things we'd spend our money on if we had the resources and were given the choice. The best way to enhance your system, of course, depends entirely on how you plan to use it. If you want to use it for instructional delivery, you'll need access to more *peripherals* and options than if you simply plan to use the system to receive courses and content from remote classrooms or professional *content provider* programs.

Additional Monitors

If a teacher camera (see page 16) is set up in the back of the classroom, an additional set of monitors also located in the back of the room allows you to view *remote sites* while you face the in-house classroom and the teacher camera. The in-house classroom, in turn, views the remote sites on the monitors in front of the room, while at the same time watching you, live, in front of the room. The cost for an additional monitor can range from $400 to $1,000, depending on the quality and size of the monitor you purchase. You may choose to use either a television monitor or some of the newer computer monitors with SVGA compatibility.

Audio Cassette/CD/DVD Player

Some IVC presenters make use of additional audio/video input, featuring tapes or discs that can be heard by the remote sites through careful placement of the microphone. We've heard of one teacher who teaches a regular class via IVC and uses a cassette player to transmit a theme song, signaling students that it's time to begin class. Audio/video input can also be accomplished through the CD or DVD player on the external computer connected to the system. The cost for this enhanced audio/video capability will range from $50 to $150.

Control Pads/Touch Pads

The basic IVC system requires use of a remote control or mouse and keyboard to access menus that enable movement between cameras and system functions. This can be time-consuming and result in a choppy presentation unless you have a technician operating the technology while you present, which is not always possible. Control tablets allow quick movement from camera to camera using push-button controls, easing considerably the technical demands on the teacher or presenter. Depending on the type of controller and features you're looking for, this kind of equipment has a wide price range: $500–$7,500. A standard control pad, however, typically costs around $750.

A typical control pad interface.

Electronic Whiteboard

When you connect this device to an IVC system, you can use it to draw diagrams or jot notes, like you would use a regular whiteboard. Electronic whiteboards also come with bells and whistles: if you select the whiteboard as a camera option, for example, you can send, in the form of a slide, to each remote site (far-site), what you've written on the board. The slide can then be downloaded as a file at the far-site, saved, and printed, or posted, on your class website. As noted previously, the electronic whiteboard can also serve as your display device for your videoconference unit. It's a nice tool for certain applications, but not strictly necessary. Cost range: $2,500–$10,000.

Teacher Camera

Generally located in the back of the room, a teacher camera captures the image of the teacher standing in front, facing the students. In a teaching situation, the teacher camera allows teachers to deliver instructions facing on-site students at the same time they face the camera that sends their image to each remote site. This is a wonderful option if you plan to present to both on-site and off-site students at the same time. This is another item with a very wide price range: $100–$4,000.

This teacher workstation has (from left) a document camera, computer, and control pad.

VCR/DVD/DV Recorder

Most IVC systems provide a video input port for use by a VCR, DVD, or digital video recorder. If you install one of these with your videoconferencing unit, you'll be able to show recorded video across the system by selecting that option on the video menu. A word of caution: video clips and films are protected by copyright and cannot always be freely transmitted in a videoconference setting, even within your school district (see Chapter 5 for more information on this). Cost: $50–$100.

Wireless Microphone and Pressure Mats

If you're the kind of teacher who likes to move around the classroom a lot, this is an ideal extra to incorporate into your IVC tool bag. The wireless microphone operates on infrared technology, allowing you to move back and forth and around the room without worrying whether you're still in the camera's sights; the camera will follow you wherever you go, within reason. A wireless microphone will cost you anywhere from $100 to $400.

Another option for teacher movement are pressure mats located on the floor in key teaching areas. When the instructor moves onto one of these mats, the camera pans to that location automatically. This option is superior to the wireless microphone because the camera isn't constantly tracking the instructor, which can cause far-site viewers to feel seasick.

All of the additional features listed in this section, if used in conjunction with the basic IVC system described in the previous section, can provide teachers and students with greatly enhanced interactive capabilities. A review (Greenberg, 2004, February) of current research on effective videoconferencing strategies in the classroom cites a study by Amirian (2003, October) that points out the critical need for interaction when using IVC as an instructional tool: "Interaction is the key component of this use of the technology to support a more social learning, negotiating meaning through interaction with peers over distance, and forming a sense of community using the technology."

A GLOBAL CLASSROOM

Duane Schade, Technology Curriculum Coordinator
Northmount School; Edmonton, Alberta, Canada

A one-room schoolhouse in Milesville, South Dakota, connects with a fourth-grade class from Holy Name School in New York City to share ideas and stories about growing up. South Dakota's K–8 students talk about places to see in South Dakota, life on the farm, cattle, and the great distances they have to travel to get to school, while NYC students talk about the city subway, Central Park, and the Statue of Liberty. Students introduce themselves, tell their ages, and indicate the profession of their parents. Initially shy, students soon begin to open up, asking questions about each other's favorite foods, games, and hobbies. Both groups of children enjoyed the experience and were disappointed when it was time to disconnect.

How IVC Works

Before we proceed, let's take a moment to reassure those of you who aren't technologists: don't be put off or bogged down by all the technical information we're about to present. It's our intention here simply to outline the basics. Though the actual network management of your IVC system will most likely be handled by your district **information technology (IT) manager,** it's nice to have a basic understanding and overview of how it all works and what some of the potential operating costs might be.

Videoconferencing involves the flow of audio and video signals through one or more telecommunication networks. All types of telecommunications involve at least one sending device that initiates the transmission of information, at least one receiving device that receives the transmission, and a communication channel that connects the two. The data or information can move through the communication channel in analog form or in digital form, or a combination of the two. An analog signal is a continuous electronic wave—which is how most telephone conversations are transmitted even today—but a digital signal consists of electronic pulses. The Internet transfers data digitally, as do fiber-optic telephone lines.

The IVC system, with the help of its codec, compresses the audio and video signals generated by the videoconference participants and sends them across a telecommunications infrastructure or network. The connection might be made via the Internet, digital or analog phone lines, or even a satellite system. Regardless of whether the sender and receiver are located across town, across the state, or even on the other side of the world, as long as the two IVC units are interoperable and run on a standards-based algorithm such as **H.323** or H.320 they'll be able to interface with each other.

If only two sites are involved, the participants can use the dial-up feature included in all systems to establish a direct connection, using either an **IP address** number or an ISDN number. An IP number indicates a location or "node" on the Internet, whereas an ISDN number is a digital phone line connection. If more than two sites will participate in the call, however, the videoconference will need to be scheduled and switched at a centralized

---

UNIVERSITY PROVIDES STATEWIDE HUB

Jack Holden, Video Conferencing and Webcasting Administrator
University of Tennessee; Knoxville, Tennessee

The University of Tennessee's Information Technology Engineering Services provides bridging services for the Vanderbilt Virtual School. Many of the sessions held so far have demonstrated the value of the program. Some of the university's campuses have also begun to reach out to public high schools for dual-credit programs. We have been able to develop an extensive videoconferencing infrastructure and expect it to grow. We also offer a robust *video streaming* (also called *streaming*) and archiving system. An infrastructure, however, is nothing without applications and content.

bridge. A bridge is often referred to as a ***multipoint control unit (MCU)*** and is a function of your local or state network's ***hub.*** Many of today's videoconference codecs include their own "mini-MCU" that allows you to connect to multiple sites, often three sites concurrently. Check with your IT specialist to determine if your unit is multisite capable.

In addition to sending and receiving audio and visual images of people, IVC technology allows teachers to transmit a variety of audiovisual materials via computer displays, document cameras, DVD players, and so forth. This miraculous method of communication takes place in real time and allows participants to interact face-to-face despite being located miles, or even continents, apart.

CONNECTING KIDS TO SPACE IN MANAOTAK

Pam Lloyd, Director
GCI SchoolAccess; Anchorage, Alaska

For several years, GCI SchoolAccess has hosted videoconferenced "visits" with astronauts and representatives from NASA. Alaska schools have used these visits to inspire students to seek careers in math and science. Sessions have included live, two-way video lessons with the Johnson Space Center in Houston, Texas. Other schools throughout surrounding areas have participated in the sessions via videoconferencing.

Astronauts have visited several schools in the Southwest Region School District to engage students in, and to promote, NASA's science and math education program. Students have enjoyed presentations from astronauts as well as live distance learning video link-ups with the International Space Station and the Johnson Space Center. Using GCI's distance learning technology, students were able to interact with astronauts, and other schools throughout surrounding areas were able to watch via videoconferencing. Students have even been able to interact live with astronauts on the International Space Station.

Network Solutions and Costs

Videoconferencing technology can operate on existing school IP **data networks** or on a statewide dedicated IP **video network**. Videoconferencing can also take place via digital phone lines (ISDN). As the rush to access virtual learning technologies picks up speed, school districts nationwide are making great strides toward improving and updating connectivity options. In many areas of the world, it's reasonable to expect to be able to operate a videoconference system over existing networks, with the exception of the cost of additional bandwidth and last mile infrastructure.

A dedicated IVC network could cost, on the state level, more than $1 million for one-time setup and installation. A monthly cost comparable to your current Internet fees could then be expected. A shared network structure adds minimal cost to your existing system, possibly requiring the expense of a larger-capacity **circuit.** Many districts have recently upgraded from T-1 capacity to **DS3** or higher.

If your school has access to **Internet2** (I-2), your network costs should be even lower. Though Internet2 is available only to education and research organizations and most states have only a handful of I-2 entry points, 38 states have formed a partnership between I-2 and K–12 schools. Some of the partnerships include bandwidth for video. For more information, check with your local state university, or visit the I-2 website (http://k20.Internet2.edu).

Some dedicated networks are run solely on ISDN connectivity. This strategy does not tap into existing IP technology but, rather, uses a digital phone line that will carry monthly charges and fees for long-distance usage. The monthly charges run approximately $100 to $400, and the line charges average $60 to $100 per hour for long-distance calls. The IP technology and the ISDN technology are interoperable through the use of a bridge, or MCU.

Bridging services are required when several IVC sites participate in a videoconference. Bridging services for a large network generally include a network scheduling system, a specially designed software program that will automatically run multiple conferences all day long.

Bridging solutions vary greatly from network to network, large and small, and are generally managed, along with the overall network, by local or state network managers. Other services that may be available through the bridge are scheduling, streaming, and video archiving. Estimated cost: $5,000 (for a small, manually operated bridge) to $300,000 (for an MCU and additional **gateway** components).

Videoconferencing networks come in many different configurations and sizes and require careful planning by network administrators. We believe that the key to successful implementation of any virtual learning system lies in the close collaboration among instructional, technology, and administrative personnel and in their ability to openly discuss needs, options, and desired outcomes and plan accordingly. We'll review the critical components of this planning process—network infrastructure, facilities design, staffing and training needs, and instructional aims—in the chapters that follow.

STUDENTS LEARN FROM TEACHER'S INSPIRATION

Lorri Fischer, Teacher
Enterprise Elementary School; Enterprise, Oregon

When I saw the advertisement for the Lewis and Clark Weekly Showcase for Teachers, a professional development opportunity available through our statewide videoconferencing network, I was intrigued. They were offering live, face-to-face lectures from Lewis and Clark scholars and from teachers who were using the Lewis and Clark theme to teach across the curriculum. I wanted to bring something like this to my classroom. After all, we are a Lewis and Clark trail state, and this was the bicentennial.

After a few weeks of meeting on the IVC network with archaeologists, scientists, and historians, I began to formulate an idea for my classroom. I was inspired! I knew the best way to understand a story is to live it, and I told my class that this was what we were going to do. Each of my fifth-grade students assumed the identity of someone who took part in the Corps of Discovery journey. Each student researched a character, and every day I gave the students a new position on their map of the journey and a new circumstance to react to and write about in their journals. We all felt as if we were part of the expedition.

Ron Osterloh's high school video production class met with my class and talked about filming certain parts of the journey. We soon began planning costumes, props, and settings. We arranged for video shoots around our small community of Enterprise, located in the Wallowa Mountains in Northeastern Oregon. The resulting video documentary starred my students, cast as members of the Lewis and Clark expedition. They really put their hearts into this. The students acted out the production for the whole community. Without access to the weekly workshops on the interactive videoconference network, we would never have had this opportunity and the inspiration it provided for the class project.

Chapter 2

Adding Value
to the
Classroom with IVC

In the educational climate created by NCLB (No Child Left Behind Act of 2001, 2002), teachers have to take a hard look at the value-added aspect of potential new instructional methods and mediums. Classroom teachers must make well-informed decisions regarding curriculum content and the use of technology tools. Though teachers are always looking for ways to improve student performance, they must also keep an eye on the bottom line and make sure they're making the best use of their resources. Videoconferencing equipment is a significant investment, and cost-effectiveness is definitely an issue that schools and districts have to consider. In this chapter, we'll take a look at the educational value of IVC and detail how both students and teachers can profit from its effective use.

In the past, classrooms were allotted a certain amount of money annually for field trips, guest speakers, and media presentations; today, those same budgets might be limited to extra classroom supplies and a trip to the local cheese factory, certainly not enough to significantly augment on-site curriculum content. An effective IVC program can help fill this budgetary void and connect students to content specialists and guest speakers, take them across the country on a ***virtual field trip,*** or provide learning partnerships with other students and teachers around the globe—in other words, add value to your classroom's learning environment not obtainable by other, more traditional, means.

Today's teachers must prepare students to be global citizens. Project-based learning is one way teachers may choose to introduce their students to global concepts. Using IVC as a project tool facilitates a more authentic opportunity for collaboration and allows students to build relationships beyond digital print. Learning through videoconferencing introduces students to their international peers and enables the teacher to scaffold new ways of knowing (Dyck, 2008). Videoconferencing enhances existing curriculum by providing avenues for both students and teachers to access resources needed to build modern skills and introduce global perspectives. From continuing education opportunities to special curriculum events, IVC technology can open doors for entire learning communities.

A first-grade class in Wessington Springs Elementary, South Dakota, receives a lesson on the weather from a fifth-grade class at Tulare Elementary. They observed demonstrations on the formation of tornadoes, hurricanes, and blizzards.

In this book, we separate IVC course and content delivery into two categories: daily classes and supplemental events. Daily IVC classes are most commonly used by schools and districts to provide students with access to highly qualified teachers and content, such as foreign language or advanced placement instruction, that the school or district cannot otherwise provide. Supplemental events, on the other hand, are one-time or limited duration events that bring students face-to-face with content experts, take them on virtual field trips, or facilitate interactive student projects and cultural exchanges with schools across the country and around the world. IVC can also be used to share with all the other schools in the district or state special resources that may exist at one school, ensuring equitable access to, and more efficient use of, those resources. Finally, educators can take advantage of videoconferencing to access for-credit and noncredit continuing education courses, as well as professional development opportunities within their field of study. In the following pages we'll explore some of the key elements and value-added possibilities of daily IVC classes, supplemental events, resource sharing, and IVC professional development.

Basic Tenets of IVC in the Classroom

Though videoconferencing in K–12 classrooms is still in the early adoption phase in many parts of the country and research on its effectiveness in the classroom is sparse, those with IVC experience agree on a few basic tenets for receiving and delivering content for students:

- The far-site, or classroom receiving the instruction, should be staffed with a classroom assistant, aka the *facilitator* (see Chapter 3).

- Teachers delivering content via IVC will spend more time planning and working through logistics than will a traditional classroom teacher (see Chapter 4).

- It is fundamental to carefully prepare all visual presentations, following guidelines for IVC media (see Chapter 5).

- *Hybrid, or blended,* courses, involving a combination of virtual education tools, yield the best results for student learning (see Chapter 6).

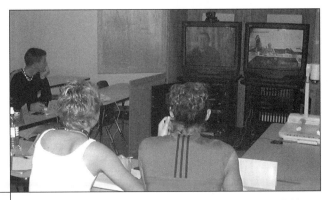

With IVC, rural schools have access to resources once available only in larger districts. Here, AP math students find a teacher.

Daily IVC Classes

Interactive videoconferencing is increasingly used in K–12 classrooms to access otherwise unavailable content for students. This application of IVC is particularly common in areas where small schools are separated by many miles. Schools sprinkled throughout the vast Midwest prairies or separated by stretches of frozen Alaskan tundra need alternative ways to provide their students with the kinds of learning opportunities and resources they'll need to meet state and federal standards. In the past, rural districts employed itinerant teachers who traveled throughout widespread districts teaching such specialized courses as advanced placement science and foreign language. Today, IVC has made it possible for far-flung schools to share highly qualified teachers and access specialized content from professional videoconferencing content providers (see Chapter 7).

Supplemental IVC Events

Access to Content Experts

It's not logistically or financially feasible to bring an astronaut into every classroom in your state or district, even though all students could benefit immeasurably from the opportunity to speak directly with someone who has been inspired to reach for the stars because of a love for science. However, IVC can make possible what would seem to be impossible!

As IVC technology has become more stable and more affordable, more students have been enabled by this two-way interactive modality to access experts at universities, science centers, museums, and even the International Space Station. They get a chance to talk with working scientists, authors, actors, artists, historians, and government officials. Most often, students walk away from these videoconferences with a broader perspective of the world and the possibilities it holds for them. IVC technology has become so popular that cameras are often built into monitors and laptops. This increased availability means students are much more comfortable using cameras than they have been in years past. Teachers should be aware of this phenomenon and teach students the appropriate use of this technology.

LIFE IN SPACE

Don Petit, an astronaut from Oregon, spoke to a group of students at the Oregon Museum of Science and Industry (OMSI) while speaking at the same time to students all around the state via the Oregon Access (IVC) Network. He told them about life aboard the International Space Station and about the importance of studying science in school.

Virtual Field Trips

Virtual field trips are a rapidly growing application of IVC technology in K–12 classrooms. Resources for traditional field trips have dwindled over the past decade, as transportation and insurance costs have risen sharply. Today, it's faster and cheaper, and sometimes more personal, to visit a museum or science center via an IVC connection. Community organizations have been quick to equip themselves with the technology to reach out to classrooms through the long arm of videoconferencing. Some early providers of virtual field trip opportunities included the Indianapolis Children's Museum, NASA, and the Los Angeles Museum of Tolerance. Today, hundreds of these organizations offer tours and presentations on thousands of topics (see Chapter 7).

Virtual field trips come in many different forms. You can take your students into the tank of a famous aquarium, across a remote field to a protected salt marsh, or into the control room of a NASA reflector telescope. Most of these virtual field trip providers are capable of connecting to your classroom via IP connectivity and will videoconference with one or more classrooms at a time. They may charge a small fee for the field trip—ranging from $50 to $300—but many are free of charge.

OHIO AUTOPSY

Gail Wheatley, Director of Electronic Education
COSI Columbus; Columbus, Ohio

COSI Columbus partnered with the Ohio State University (Columbus) Pathology Department and 20 teachers to create a program called In Depth: Autopsy. This program encourages students to learn about pathology and autopsies prior to the videoconference. During the videoconference, students watch a taped autopsy narrated by a forensic pathologist. They can ask questions of the pathologist during the videoconference, pursuing the topics that most interest them. After the videoconference, students are required to determine cause of death by conducting toxicology tests, interpreting the results of a toxicology report and examining histology slides. Students write a final autopsy report, supporting their conclusions with data and evidence.

COSI collaborated with 20 high school teachers in seven different states to develop the program. These teachers helped guide development and offered opinions and concerns via e-mail and videoconference meetings. They reviewed all teacher materials and tried all activities before they were finalized. The teachers that were within an hour's driving distance of COSI also allowed the COSI team to observe their students testing the program and all its activities, further strengthening the activities. In Depth: Autopsy was created through strong collaborations with professionals in the fields of both pathology and education. The strength and synergy of collaboration are clearly evident in the program and the interest students take in it.

When searching for a virtual field trip for your class, we recommend asking providers ahead of time if their IVC programs for students conform with state or federal standards. Ask detailed questions about what they offer and what to expect during a videoconference. You might even ask other videoconferencing teachers if they have had an experience with the virtual field trip program that they would recommend for your class.

University School of Nashville astronomy students chat with Vanderbilt Dyer Observatory Director Rick Chappell about the sun and its influence on the planets.

AROUND THE STATE IN 60 MINUTES

Christie Rickert, Distance Learning Specialist
Hays CISD; Hays, Texas

To enhance the fourth-grade social studies curriculum, students throughout Texas connect for a collaborative project titled Around the State in 60 Minutes. Students in "mystery regions" of Texas connect via videoconferencing to present their region in many creative and unique formats. They work together to plan presentations such as game shows, including regional facts, impersonations of significant regional explorers, mock newscasts about the region, and entertaining yet informative skits.

Students not only have to communicate facts about their own region, but they also have to practice listening, and using critical-thinking skills, as they evaluate other class presentations and try to predict where in the state the other mystery regions are located. Students have the opportunity to ask clarifying questions of each presenting class and make inferences before announcing their final predictions about the mystery regions of Texas.

In October 2007, Texas teachers, librarians, technologists, and Education Service Center specialists made it possible for more than 700 Texas fourth-graders to travel, virtually, Around the State in 60 Minutes.

What better way to learn about the regions of Texas than to interact with the kids that live there?

Interactive Student Projects

Videoconferencing allows K–12 teachers to step back and let their students interact with each other and use equipment in pursuit of their own learning experience. Like your own, the students' ability to use the technology will develop over time and is often fostered through traditional applications. Interactive projects extend cooperative learning experiences, allowing them to work with others from different cultures and backgrounds around the globe. Students soon realize they can learn much more about the subject matter when they participate in these types of interactive projects. They're likely to take to the technology quickly and may need guidance only on etiquette and protocol issues.

Interactive student projects might take the form of labs, panels, or a cooperative project-based group. An IVC lab project could be a simple, inquiry-based science lesson. Students in two, or even three, distant locations have used IVC to investigate the temperature at which water boils, discovering that water boils at different temperatures depending on altitude and other geographical variables.

Student panels might interact with college or university students to find out what college life is really like and what they need to accomplish in high school to prepare themselves for success in college. They might also discuss pressing topics such as dorm life and other social opportunities. The discussion often becomes quite lively, and students quickly forget their reservations about being in front of the camera. IVC enables them to make an easy connection with college students they might never have the opportunity to interact with otherwise. As always, there's no better teacher than one's peers!

Cooperative groups of K–12 students might work together on a common area of study, such as geography, sharing information about their own corner of the world. A content provider group in the state of Washington developed a videoconferencing project called "Where in Washington?" Student participants around the state must guess where other participants are located based on the geographical and cultural clues provided by the other students. Off-camera research is conducted by participating students before the final answer to the question is provided by each group.

ANTHRAX EXPERTS

During the anthrax scare in 2001, students around the United States interacted via IVC with infectious disease doctors at Vanderbilt University Medical Center to learn more about this bioterrorism threat and other related topics.

FUTURE FARMERS

High school students in Oregon used their statewide IVC network after school and talked to high school students around the state about their accomplishments as members of Future Farmers of America. They dispelled myths about FFA and talked with pride about national conference awards they won for service, public speaking, and numerous AgEd projects. The remote students had lots of questions, and when it was over, all the students went home having learned about student leadership opportunities, this unique technology, and each other.

CRUCIAL IVC CONVERSATIONS

Ruth Litman-Block, Director
Virtual Learning Center; Cooperating School Districts; St. Louis, Missouri

For the past eight years, CSD in St. Louis has been conducting a series of five videoconference dialogues between three to four high schools on the topic of race relations and racism. High school students from different demographic areas of the St. Louis metropolitan area (urban, suburban, and rural), as well as other locations in the United States, have had an opportunity to talk with each other during this series of dialogues. The objectives of the program are:

- To explore students' personal attitudes about racism and race relations

- To increase students' awareness about racism and race relations in their schools and communities

- To increase students' awareness about institutional racism

- To encourage dialogue between high schools about eliminating racism and improving race relations

- To empower high school students to become change agents around the issues of racism in their schools and communities

Each IVC session deals with a different aspect of the topic. Here is the breakdown:

- Session 1—Developing a common language to talk about racism, stereotyping, discrimination, and prejudice.

- Session 2—What I learned growing up.

- Session 3—How inclusive is my school?

- Session 4—What procedures and policies would make my school more inclusive?

- Session 5—What can I personally do to change things?

Led by a professional facilitator from A World of Difference Institute, a division of the Anti-Defamation League, students have a chance to share their perspectives, ideas, concerns, and dreams for creating more inclusive school environments. They also share visions for more inclusive communities in which to live.

Students are asked to develop and implement action plans designed to improve race relations and interrupt racism in their schools and in their regions. Students who have participated in the past have shared some very disturbing incidents of discrimination that they, personally, have experienced, such as being tracked into certain courses just on the basis of the previous school district they attended and the color of their skin.

One of the greatest outcomes one year was the establishment of a monthly Culture Day in one of the high schools. This was a day when one culture was celebrated, and students in that culture had an opportunity to bring in food, clothing, and customs to share with the student body. Students created this program as a direct result of their action plan in the IVC dialogues. They presented it to their administrators, who then implemented it.

We've heard great stories about high school teams debating via IVC, musical performances shared between remote high school orchestras, and students sharing information with each other regarding student council or other student leadership programs. This kind of student-to-student interaction is immensely powerful and rewarding.

Members of the Dakota Wind Quintet perform a musical selection during a concert at Baltic High School. The event uses IVC to expand the audience and provides a valuable musical enrichment activity for students. (Photo by Brian Dzwonek)

BEST PRACTICES

In a white paper titled "Best Practices in Live Content Acquisition by Distance Learning Organizations," Alan Greenberg and Russ Colbert (2002) note three stages in the process of deploying IVC in the classroom:

1. During the first stage, deployment tends to stay within the district, where users share limited resources and teacher training, and support administrative meetings.

2. In the second stage, the technology becomes a tool for accessing content or cultural exchanges outside the district.

3. Finally, a district or individual school becomes adept at delivering its own programs to others.

If you're interested in these ideas and want to search for other classrooms to share student collaborations, look around your own district and state or post queries on national IVC e-mail lists. Many other teachers are in search of virtual classroom partnership opportunities both in your state and around the globe. Some states host a clearinghouse for teachers and students seeking to collaborate with other teachers and students on a specific topic. Following are two websites serving the worldwide educational IVC community:

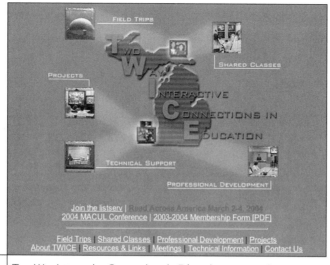

Two Way Interactive Connections in Education: www.twice.cc

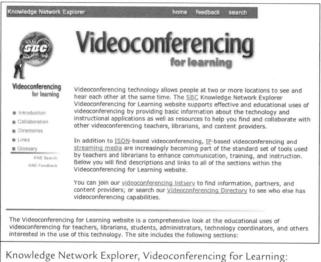

Knowledge Network Explorer, Videoconferencing for Learning:
www.kn.pacbell.com/wired/vidconf/vidconf.html

Resource Sharing

More and more school districts across the country are looking for ways to take advantage of virtual learning to fill the gaps in their teaching staff. An obvious and cost-effective videoconferencing application for districts, or even for statewide education systems, is the sharing of instructional resources. For example, in order to meet the needs of high school students and solve the problem of limited staff, a small rural district may share, district-wide, via IVC, one Spanish teacher or physics teacher. This doesn't mean teachers' jobs will be lost, or open positions left unfilled; it means no students will be left behind because of a shortage of resources. In many states, specialized teachers in high demand are shared, via IVC technology, with districts across the state.

Of course, there are issues to be overcome when students from different schools or districts share one teacher. Bell schedules may conflict, discipline guidelines may differ, and instructional expectations may not be what students are used to. But none of these cultural or logistical differences is so complicated that it can't be overcome. The desire to make use of the technology to serve students will help with these challenges. To solve the bell-schedule issues, some schools have implemented a zero period distance-education schedule, allowing students to meet for IVC classes before the school day begins. Some have even cooperated to align conflicting schedules. We believe there are more solutions than there are problems.

Students from McCook Central High School in Salem, South Dakota, discuss proper diapering technique as part of the parenting class offered by the Emery School District. (Photo by Brian Dzwonek)

Professional Development

Interactive videoconferencing also offers numerous benefits and opportunities for teachers. The technology opens a door to the world and provides teachers with chances to:

- Attend meetings
- Collaborate with other teachers
- Continue their formal education
- Observe other classrooms/students

Imagine you've been appointed to a state-level committee, but you know there's no way you're going to be able to attend the meetings in your capital city 250 miles away. You wouldn't dream of asking your principal for time off, funds for travel, or a substitute teacher. But videoconferencing is available in your district, and it's also available in the State Board of Education room where the meetings will take place. Now you can attend— and even impress other participants with your technological savvy.

READ AROUND THE PLANET

Janine Lim, Instructional Technology Consultant
Berrien RESD; Berrien Springs, Michigan

Imagine your students connecting with peers around the world to celebrate reading. Every year since 2002, TWICE (Two Way Interactive Connections in Education) has coordinated Read Around the Planet, formerly named Read Across America. In early March, K–12 classes are matched to celebrate reading. In 2006, the project was piloted with Alberta, Canada, and the United Kingdom, and it has been an international project since then. More than 1,300 classes participated in 2007, including classes from Canada, the United Kingdom, Taiwan, and Nicaragua. This quote from sixth-grade teacher Shane Grundy, of Edmonton, Alberta, sums up the quality of this conference.

> In my school I coordinated nine different connections—all between Canada and the United States. Each time, students were amazed to discover that despite the different flags and weather patterns, we are all the same. Children thousands of kilometers away play just like children in Canada do. They, too, love recess and hate math. They, too, study hard and play harder. Each time I disconnected from the remote site the first reaction was always "Wow! They're just like us." It didn't matter if they were kindergarten or Grade 6, mainstream, learning strategies, or an alternative program, they all reacted the same. My students all knew they had just made a connection to people a world away, and they were just like them.
>
> Everyone has a different story to tell, we all walk different paths; but in the end, people are people, no matter where they're from, the colour of their skin, the anthem they sing, or the grade they're in. People are people. I can't think of a better lesson to teach our students, or a better way to teach it.

Please visit www.twice.cc/read/ for more information.

The Benefits—Something for Everyone

Videoconferencing technology serves entire school communities, providing classes and supplemental events for students of all ages and serving teachers with even a minimum of technological skills. When students gain access to critical curriculum content, they are no longer at risk of being left behind. When students are given the chance to interact with specialists from around the world, the boundaries of their school or community are removed, and they open themselves to experiences that will remain with them for the rest of their lives. Similarly, when teachers become familiar and comfortable with IVC technologies, they are enabled to participate in professional development workshops and degree-enhancing classes. In the real-life stories that follow, you will have a chance to see how IVC can uniquely benefit the entire community.

IVC enables students to access otherwise unavailable classes. Videoconferencing promotes equal opportunity learning by providing all learners access to courses no matter where these learners are located and no matter what kinds of teaching or material resources are available to them in their home communities.

In a small mountain-valley community, the school year was about to begin, and no Spanish teacher was on board for high school students. Even though Spanish was a much-needed class, the superintendent was painfully aware few options were available to solve the problem. One of their neighboring communities had just hired a Spanish teacher, and the superintendent in the mountain-valley community began to consider the possibility of making use of his community's recently installed videoconferencing system. After several conversations, meetings, technology-troubleshooting sessions, completion of a two-hour training session for the neighboring community's Spanish teacher, and assignment of an on-site teacher/facilitator at the mountain-valley high school, the superintendent announced the availability of Spanish I and II for their students.

Having never used the technology on a daily basis, they had to iron out many glitches after the class began. The teacher invested many long hours in planning and troubleshooting. They were surprised, however, that students remained positive throughout the growing pains. They said such things as, "We like going to class with kids at other schools," and, "It's neat to see yourself on TV!" The students would not have had access to this critical content without the implementation of the IVC program.

IVC broadens students' view of the world. Students are not restricted by time and place when they have access to IVC. People, places, objects, and ideas that students might not otherwise encounter are available remotely, allowing students to expand their knowledge on a particular subject, learn more about the world, and meet peers beyond classroom and community borders.

The distance learning program series from Indiana University's International Programs provides a collaboration activity among four elementary schools, bringing together three curriculum areas: social studies, science, and art. Teachers choose three world environments (South American rainforest, Canadian Arctic, and Chinese bamboo forest) for their students to study. The students visit the Indianapolis Zoo interactively three times to learn about animals in each of the environments. Then they connect to experts at Indiana University three times to learn about the human culture in each of the environments, focusing on how the local animals are integrated into the culture. To culminate the unit, each student creates a picture of one of the animals in a culturally appropriate art form. "Our program uses interactive video technology to connect K–12 schools and community groups in Indiana and other states with university international students, scholars, and specialists," says Kathleen Sobiech.

IVC increases student motivation for learning. Videoconferencing, say many K–12 practitioners, can be a motivator for students. Doors are opened for students to interact with positive role models throughout the world. In the case of a guest speaker who is a specialist in a particular field of study, for example, students have a chance to interact with someone who has devoted his or her life to this work, and that passion and enthusiasm is contagious. The infusion of IVC technology can engage students in core curricular subjects while broadening the context of their learning.

Southmont High School students in Crawfordsville, Indiana, hear a career presentation from attorney Dan Taylor. Students in other parts of the state participate via IVC through CILC, the Center for Interactive Learning and Collaboration.

"We have a very active theater arts group here at Jackson High School (in Massilon, Ohio)," explains teacher Marsha Weaver, the school's distance learning coordinator. "Our students have received rave reviews for the plays and musicals they perform. Our theater arts teachers wanted to put the students to the test, so we connected with Arts 4 All through videoconferencing and participated in their Brush Up Your Shakespeare program. Our students had the opportunity to perform for the other participating schools and a celebrity panel, made up of TV and movie stars.

"After the performance everyone was very quiet. The teachers looked at me and then to the students, then to the big screen, where the panel sat motionless and wide-eyed. Finally, both the panel and the teachers began to clap and shout out how wonderful the performance was. Our students were asked to 'Do it again!' And again, everyone applauded. What an unbelievable feeling of accomplishment our students felt. They would not have been able to get this type of feedback without the great wonder of videoconferencing."

IVC enriches the existing curriculum. Many ways exist to turn a good lesson into a spectacular lesson, and a well-planned videoconference is one of them. Just as in the past a guest speaker or a field trip would highlight and enrich a unit of study, an IVC event can accomplish the same goal.

"Getting students excited about history can be challenging," says Barbara Laudicina, principal of Doyle Elementary School in Fair Lawn, New Jersey. "Several years ago, while teaching about the Revolutionary War to fifth-graders at Warren Point School in Fair Lawn, I decided to take them on a virtual trip to England. With videoconferencing equipment at my disposal, we began to cultivate a relationship with a teacher and his students in Lincoln, England. Our students became e-pals and were soon introduced via videoconference. In light of the five-hour time difference, we were greeted at our first session with 'Good afternoon!' We responded, 'Good morning!'

"Students at both sites worked in cooperative groups to research their communities, and then they turned to the Revolutionary War, or the 'American War' as it is referred to in England. Time lines and cause and effect charts were developed and shared. Finally, our English counterparts provided us with an expert on the British foot soldier of Lexington and Concord. Appearing in period uniform, he quipped that it was believed that a colonist fired 'the shot heard around the world.' My students fired back that, according to American sources, no one knows who shot first. We all laughed and then agreed that either was certainly possible. Our unique journey provided us with an enhanced perspective that no text could provide."

Students from the Fralin Biotechnology Center of Virginia Tech University get a kick out of hearing Blue Ridge Virtual Governor's School students sing about the results of their genetics experiments.

IVC provides just-in-time learning environments. Videoconferencing affords students the opportunity to dialogue with real people who have lived through historic events around the world. Whether the person they are talking with is a World War II veteran or an expert on a recent world event, time is an important factor. Students are able to ask questions and inquire about global events in a "just-in-time" learning environment.

A Bridging the Gap connection with the Museum of Tolerance in Los Angeles brought the Holocaust to life for Marsha Weaver's students. "This was the most moving and inspiring connection we have ever experienced," she says. "There is no way that a classroom teacher could instill the trials and tribulations expressed by this person. At one point during the connection I looked around our lab (which seats 70) and noticed that most of the girls were wiping tears from their eyes and the boys were dead silent, with their eyes glued on our presenter. The world became much smaller for those students that day. Several of the students went home after the videoconference and called their grandparents, aunts, and uncles to find out more about what they might know about the Holocaust. The Bridging the Gap connection opened more than classroom doors to our students; it opened doors for students to learn from their relatives. What an awesome experience made available only through videoconferencing."

Students at St. George's Academy listen raptly to the story of Menachem
Limor, a survivor of Buchenwald concentration camp.

IVC provides opportunities for teachers to collaborate. Teachers are no longer isolated
in school buildings and classrooms because IVC allows them to collaborate with other
teachers in their districts, regions, and across their state. In school systems that are spread
out across many miles or across town, in both rural and urban areas, curriculum directors
can meet, via videoconference, from three or four locations at a time.

Some high schools in North Carolina have only one chemistry teacher to serve many
students, explains Carole Stern, chemistry instructor at the North Carolina School of
Science and Mathematics in Durham. In these schools, the difficulty in locating a mentor
for an inexperienced chemistry teacher can be overcome by videoconferencing.

Stern explains: "During the 2000–2001 school year, seven freshly minted chemistry
teachers from across the state joined hour-long biweekly videoconferences with veteran
chemistry teacher Myra Halpin. The new teachers were looking for guidance on how to
pace a Chemistry I class in order to cover the North Carolina Standard Course of Study
and prepare their students for the state's standardized End of Course test. Participants
also wanted to see how to set up and conduct labs and demonstrations to address particular learning objectives. Later, these teachers reported that what they valued most in the
IVC workshop were the conversations and presentations that helped them develop their
own bag of tricks, and explanations for teaching hard-to-understand concepts."

Three years have passed and Halpin reports that she continues to hear from these teachers.
They ask her for assistance in offering advanced placement chemistry in their schools.
They would like to meet again via an after-school videoconference series to interact and
learn from her as they did before. Says one teacher, "I was a first-year (lateral entry) teacher,
and Dr. Halpin made me wonder why I didn't start teaching 32 years ago. She made the
subject come alive."

IVC provides continuing education opportunities for teachers. Teachers also need to take
continuing education courses or acquire advanced degrees to be classified as "highly
qualified" in every course they teach. Many first-year or beginning teachers worry about
accepting positions in remote areas where they won't be able to access university classes.
However, IVC classes are now available in many teacher education programs throughout
the country.

IVC is great for enabling teachers to further their education in such ways as enrolling in distance learning classes through Vanderbilt University.

In rural Oregon, teachers are able to take classes toward a master's degree in education using their local school IVC sites to connect to the statewide videoconferencing network. The classes are provided by Eastern Oregon University, La Grande, Oregon, at a variety of remote locations. Without this opportunity, these professionals would not have the chance to advance their degrees because of the hundreds of miles separating them and the university campus. These programs are also augmented by online classes, providing even more options for teachers to continue their education while still working in the classroom.

IVC provides professional development opportunities.
Teachers can attend workshops and participate in regional and national initiatives without leaving their schools. The use of IVC eliminates the price of travel for both presenters and participants.

South Dakota has used videoconferencing to provide professional development to schools, explains state employee Rita Hitchcock. During the Technology for Teaching and Learning Academies, participants used two-way videoconferencing in a variety of ways: to deliver content to multiple sites and participants, to foster collaboration between teachers working on projects at different locations, to train instructors and conduct organizational meetings for various academies, and to showcase technology units implemented in each school's curriculum.

Coordinated School Health used the videoconference system as a delivery method for a yearlong professional development course targeted at teachers. The class met once a month and focused on different topics related to health issues. Experts were able to connect via the network to bring expertise, interest, and knowledge to the program. More than 200 teachers participated, some earning graduate credit.

CILC

The Center for Interactive Learning and Collaboration (CILC) offers many professional development opportunities for K–12 teachers, delivered over IVC. Topics include curricular offerings, teaching methods, and best practices. They also offer "Spotlight" sessions, which are online webinars. To check on current offerings, visit www.cilc.org and look under CILC Consulting Services. A typical workshop topic list might include:

- The Myth of Homework: Examining Current Practice, Research, and Alternatives.

- Comprehension Development for Beginning Readers

- Content-Area Reading (by Dr. Chris Accetturo)

- Raising Achievement by Raising Confidence: Help for Struggling Math Students

- Professional Development: Distance Learning and Your Curriculum

PROFESSIONAL DEVELOPMENT, NORTH CAROLINA STYLE

Darlene Haught; Dean, Distance Learning Technologies
North Carolina School of Science & Mathematics; Raleigh, North Carolina

The Collaboration Experience is a professional development program that partners experienced teachers at the North Carolina School of Science and Mathematics (NCSSM) with teachers at distant high schools around the state. NCSSM teachers help the high school teachers integrate technology, experience discovery-based learning, and find new approaches to teaching difficult topics.

The program, offered through NCSSM's Distance Learning Department, uses IVC to mentor new teachers, providing them with effective teaching strategies, a better understanding of pedagogy, and a wealth of resources for their own classroom use. Working together to set pacing for course content and a structure for communication, they also meet together with the distant site class via IVC, allowing the mentor teacher to either teach the class, modeling effective instructional strategies, or observe the teacher teaching the class.

The Collaboration is not designed to evaluate these teachers but to build a relationship that can expand into a network of teachers sharing best practices and new ideas.

Please visit www.dlt.ncssm.edu/distance_learning for more information.

Measuring Results

Educators are assessors. They look at how students learn and what tools or modifications should be employed to make the learning experience more beneficial. Whenever teachers integrate a new technology, they, and the administrators who support them, inevitably look for a way to measure the results, to prove that the technology is actually benefiting students and increasing their performance and knowledge. While we believe that technology should never be the focus of classroom instruction—it should, instead, be seen as a tool or mechanism that enables learning in useful ways—we don't believe that a given technology's effect on learning can be accurately measured in isolation from other factors that make up a particular learning environment. However, the hard reality is that funding for any technology or other instructional support mechanism will dry up if measurable results are not identified.

It's not uncommon for adopters of new technologies and new education paradigms to make the mistake of looking for measurable results during the first few months or years of implementation. Distance education technologies in particular should be given a wide berth for success, given the fact that they are so different from traditional instructional delivery methods. Teachers must be trained and given the opportunity to gain experience over time. Students need time to catch on to new ways of learning and interacting with virtual learning tools. When planning a new IVC program, then, ample time should be allowed for this fluency to develop.

Unfortunately, the focus of politicians and educational reformers today is almost entirely on improving standardized test scores as the sole measurement of student achievement. Given this political climate, what role can videoconferencing play in raising test scores? We believe IVC can do a lot in this regard, even though we currently lack the comprehensive statistical evidence required by NCLB mandates. That evidence will come, but for now we can offer the following argument: Because standardized tests require that students in all parts of the country demonstrate the same basic skills and standards of performance—no matter where they live or what resources they have available to them in their local schools and communities—the burden is on teachers to ensure that their students have acquired this knowledge base. Videoconferencing can help them expand their curriculum and broaden the scope of learning experiences so that their students develop a greater understanding of core curriculum concepts and more facility in applying them when answering exam questions. Videoconferencing provides students with resources they are not likely to have access to in real life (Branzburg, 2001).

Even though we think IVC should clearly have a place in districts' plans for meeting NCLB standards, we also believe that the true educational value of IVC should be measured in number and quality of learning opportunities, not test scores. In his recent literature review, Greenberg (2004, February) concludes that "...this technology is vital for expanding student access to a wealth of instruction, and...videoconferencing can be seen as a remarkably useful tool when combined with robust, well-planned, student-centered instruction" (p. 22).

IVC helps students meet standardized testing requirements. Here, students visit with Lewis and Clark scholars.

Videoconferencing is not a silver bullet. Like any other technology, it's not going to raise student test scores by itself or save districts piles of money, particularly in the short term. As a long-term investment, however, it is an unbeatable tool for accessing resources and expanding curricular offerings. Videoconferencing makes it possible to:

- Eliminate restrictions normally created by time and geography

- Bring high-price speakers to your school for little or no cost

- Provide students with highly qualified teachers and advanced placement classes that would otherwise be unavailable

- Enhance achievement of core curriculum content standards

- Allow students to observe professionals in the workplace

- Create classroom partnerships with students in other schools across the country and around the world

IVC Investment from a Cost/Benefit Perspective

Many K–12 educators are stymied by a basic misunderstanding of the costs and procedures involved in using videoconferencing technologies. Though you may be excited about the potential for videoconferencing in your school, you may first need to convince your superintendent, principal, parents, and other teachers. If you already have videoconferencing technology available in your school, you may need to use the information in these pages to help solicit support to actually utilize the technology.

As noted in Chapter 1, deployment and implementation of a videoconference network includes a wide range of equipment and infrastructure costs. It's critical that IT managers, curriculum directors, teachers, and administrators work together closely to formulate a plan that works for your school and community.

With the recent emergence of low-cost IVC solutions, the critical investment is in teacher and support staff training and follow-up professional development. Many districts now employ technology leaders and technology facilitators, who are available to support classroom teachers as they implement new technologies in the classroom. Working with on-site or district technology staff reduces the cost of off-site professional development programs.

In the course of writing this book, we conducted an informal survey of states vigorously pursuing virtual learning systems for PK–16 learners, libraries, and health care systems and found that the most successful and accessible programs

- are funded by state legislatures;

- are funded as part of basic education services;

- are now supported nationwide, in rural areas by Department of Agriculture Rural Utility Service grants; and

- are enhancing state and local funding with grants, fees for services, and E-rate funding.

Furthermore, the following factors seem to have a determinant effect on the successful implementation of these programs:

- The state Department of Education takes a leadership role.

- Centralized management is provided by higher education, state-level education organizations, or state government network managers.

- Centralized funding and management of a single, reliable network ensures equal access for everyone and enables states to purchase capacity and equipment at discounts.

- Content development programs are primarily provided by nonprofit education organizations.

Examples of major infrastructure investment include the state of Washington, where in 1996 state legislators authorized $55 million to build the K–20 Educational Telecommunications Network. MOREnet, a statewide educational IVC program started at the University of Missouri, is funded at 60% by the state through a direct appropriation to the university, and at 40% through E-rate and customer fees (based on numbers of certified FTE at each participating site). Similarly, Oklahoma provided (through a voter-approved bond issue) $14 million for the start-up of OneNet, run by the State Board of Regents and now supported by annual membership fees. Fees paid by out-of-state users now fully support the Florida Virtual School, whose start-up costs were paid for by the state.

> ## ACCESS FOR ALL
>
> "Like the highway system, this infrastructure investment is essential to meet a major public need. The public will democratize access to knowledge. The gap between information rich and information poor will be greatly reduced as access to the new learning technologies is provided to all Illinoisans regardless of where they live, work, or learn."
>
> —Illinois Century Network
> www.illinois.net/about/vision.htm

E-rate remains a crucial component in the technology funding equation. E-rate is a federally funded discount program for telecommunications services provided to schools and libraries. It was established by the Telecommunications Act of 1996. Many states apply for the discount program as a consortium of schools administered by state departments of education or other state agencies. Each participating school district is required to submit technology plans that must be approved. E-rate guidelines change from year to year, and it's likely an expert on the state level is available where you're located. To obtain direct information about E-rate funding, visit the Universal Service Administrative Company website (www.sl.universalservice.org).

In recent years, IVC product vendors have stepped up to the plate to help schools identify appropriate grants assistance programs that match the characteristics of their school districts. Both Polycom and TANDBERG have grants assistance programs to help K–12 schools. Visit their websites for more information.

Is IVC worth the cost? Videoconferencing costs are not, and will never be, cheap; but we believe the potential benefits clearly outweigh the expenditures. If you were to compare the expense of organizing an on- or off-site professional development workshop for an entire faculty with an IVC conference between faculty and content experts—with no travel involved for either side—the cost-effectiveness of the technology becomes obvious. Providing access to courses required by colleges but not available to students without the use of videoconferencing may be a priceless contribution toward a student's successful application to a university. And expanding the view a student has of the world without charging for a field trip makes the cost of the technology inconsequential. In a recent IVC symposium held by the Regional Technology Education Centers (RTEC), a resounding number of participants—representing content providers, end users, and state and regional administrators—agreed that "the value of the learning opportunities is worth the cost" (Holznagel, 2003).

A study conducted in Alberta, Canada (Anderson, 2008), indicates a sound rationale for purchasing IVC technologies for administration and for professional development. Another report (Alberta Education, 2006) had this to say about videoconferencing:

> Videoconferencing technology was observed to enhance regular classroom delivery by allowing students to engage in learning activities with peers, experts, and other educational resources outside of their traditional classroom. Students generally enjoyed these enrichment activities and seemed eager to expand their learning opportunities using the technology. The technology also fit with some inquiry-based learning designs and allowed students to interact first hand with experts and remote students with particular skills and interests. These enrichment activities were wide ranging and included linkages with students in other regions of Canada and internationally. In an era marked by pervasive networking, exposing students, educators, and administrators to the skills they need for effective use of these emerging learning and communications technologies not only enhances their performance and motivation, but also empowers them with lifelong learning skills and experiences.

> While videoconferencing technology can play an important role in adding immediacy to distance education delivery, when used alone it does not appear to provide as rich an environment as one in which various tools and techniques are blended to create more engaging and effective learning experiences. The research team concluded that videoconferencing technology alone provided only a relatively limited set of interactions, and that it should be enhanced with other networked learning tools, both synchronous and asynchronous, to increase educational efficacy. These tools could include webconferencing, e-mail, blogs, computer-conferencing, use of individualized learning objects, collaborative work project spaces, web searches and e-portfolios. (p. 5)

The increased availability of videoconferencing in schools permits teachers to take advantage of the benefits of this technology by establishing an expanded community of learners (Martin, 2005).

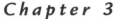

Chapter 3

Getting Started with IVC

Introducing new technology into the classroom requires more than buying equipment, plugging it in, and turning it on. Although that's a good first step, much more is required to integrate a new instructional delivery system seamlessly into your curriculum and pedagogy. In a perfect world, of course, everything teachers would need in order to learn to use one of these *emerging technologies* would be on hand as soon as initial purchases are made. But because of funding shortfalls and high competition for dwindling technology dollars, this hardly ever happens.

This chapter will help you establish a certain baseline familiarity with IVC technologies, including facilities, equipment, staffing, and training required to work well in an educational setting. We'll outline what you need in order to send and receive content, access remote opportunities, and collaborate with colleagues across the miles.

Leishawn Spotted Bear from the Fort Worth (Texas) Museum of Science and History discusses interesting adaptations; and students from Joshua, Texas, engage in an owl pellet dissection during an Adaptation Exploration—Owls program.

Facilities

Program Planning and Facilities Design

Designing a virtual learning facility can be tremendous fun. However, when you get started, remember to keep an eye on the projected instructional use rather than on the technology's bells and whistles. Will you be teaching a math class to remote students, or will you be receiving, from a remote teacher, a foreign language class for students in your building? Will you be using the facility for a variety of purposes, both sending and receiving? Once you have an instructional plan in place (see Chapter 4 for planning ideas), you can design a facility and incorporate the pieces of equipment that will best suit everyone's needs without breaking the budget. Above all, avoid starting off by saying something like, "I just love the whiteboard function. What can I teach so that I can use a whiteboard in the lesson?" Instruction begins with objectives and ends with assessment; technology should not drive those kinds of decisions. Instead, the facility and the equipment should be seen as tools that can support the achievement of these instructional goals.

The same rules apply to the design of the videoconferencing classroom. Ask yourself: How will this IVC facility best meet the needs of all those who will be using it? How can it be designed to support the kinds of instruction you and your peers have planned?

Preparation is key to a successful videoconferencing session, including arrangement of furniture.

Key elements to consider when planning a virtual learning classroom include the following:

1. The classroom design and technology configuration should be conducive to learning and instruction.

2. The location of the virtual learning facility should be accessible to everyone who will use it; designated IVC classrooms or labs are optimal. The facility should have direct access to network infrastructure and/or ISDN phone lines.

3. The environment (lighting/acoustics) should support effective videoconferencing.

Support for Learning and Instruction

The virtual learning classroom or lab should be functional and comfortable, as well as large enough for the number of people who will typically use it. For effective learning and instruction to occur, it should be designed to support optimal ***two-way interaction.*** Technology should never overrun a classroom. Monitors and cameras should be wall mounted when possible to reduce the amount of floor space lost to equipment carts. Safety is also an issue when myriad media carts fill the room. If at all possible, for optimal flexibility the instructor's workstation should be a mobile cart with a laptop, document camera, and camera controls. Allow for some empty space in the classroom where students can gather as a group in front of the camera to give presentations, debate, or participate with remote sites in collaborative projects.

Location

For ease of use by the teaching staff, the best location for an IVC system is a dedicated virtual learning classroom. However, because of limited space in many K–12 schools, this isn't always possible. Alternative scenarios might include a fixed location in a science lab, a library media center, or even an individual classroom. Whatever the location, it should meet the basic requirements of effective videoconferencing (see Chapter 5).

While most room-sized IVC units are fixed in one location, mobile systems can be rolled from classroom to classroom as long as **data ports** or ISDN lines are available in each room. Fixed locations are generally the best choice if a limited number of ISDN lines come into a school. Fixed locations reduce the stress of unplugging and reconnecting equipment, and when a classroom has the equipment fully installed and ready to go, teachers are more likely to use the technology on a regular basis. On the other hand, if the district has sufficient bandwidth and IP videoconferencing is possible, mobile carts can be an excellent instructional resource. Much like the computer cart in the early 1980s, the mobile IVC cart allows any classroom in the school to have access to this technology. It also avoids the difficulty and inconvenience of setting up and scheduling a dedicated videoconferencing room. One concern, however, is the unavoidable wear and tear on equipment; rolling equipment down school corridors often reduces the life span of the unit.

The Videoconferencing Environment

To achieve expedient participation for all end users of a videoconference, elements such as lighting, acoustics, and visuals should be taken into account. If at all possible, the videoconference room should be carpeted, draped, and located away from noisy areas such as gymnasiums, cafeterias, boiler rooms, and congested hallways. A dropped ceiling will help absorb noise. Diffused lighting will assist in limiting monitor glare. Walls should be painted a soft pastel. The room itself shouldn't be cluttered. A plain backdrop will provide a pleasing picture for remote-site participants.

The salespeople who supply your IVC equipment are often a good source of free advice for this sort of planning and will be eager to help you make wise decisions about the design and implementation of your virtual education classroom.

Virtual Classroom Setup

It's important to configure your classroom so that students and teachers can easily view the far-site and the far-site can easily view students and teachers at your site, facilitating optimal face-to-face interaction. Careful consideration should be paid to seating, camera, microphone, and monitor placement. If peripherals such as document cameras or electronic whiteboards will be used, they should be situated for ease of access by the teacher and students. "There are as many variations in [IVC] room designs, configurations, layouts, and seating arrangements as there are differences among schools, classrooms, teachers, and learning styles. As might be expected, some work better than others. But there are basic principles and guidelines which are common to those that do" (Foshee, 1997).

The following diagrams feature three potential IVC classroom setups:

Diagram 1 illustrates a traditional classroom setup, with students seated in rows or clusters and facing the front of the classroom. The instructional area is located in the front of the room, with the teacher located just to the right of the instructional area. A monitor mounted to the wall in the corner of the classroom allows students to view the remote site, and the IVC unit (which may include another monitor) is on a cart positioned under the wall-mounted monitor. Computers may also be located in the front of the classroom, near the instructional area. One disadvantage of this configuration is that little space is available for small-group or collaborative-project presentations to far-sites.

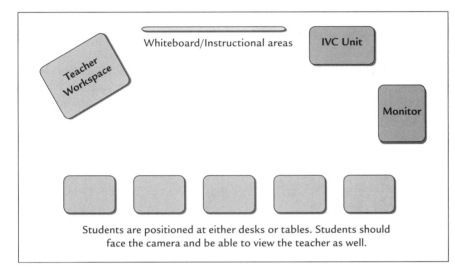

DIAGRAM 1

Another effective configuration is the horseshoe design, in which the students' desks are arranged in a semicircle and the IVC unit is placed at the open end of the horseshoe (see Diagram 2). This creates a sense of inclusion and community for both local and remote participants. This configuration lends itself to flexible instruction and collaboration because the teacher and students can present from almost any location in the classroom.

The horseshoe design creates a sense of community.

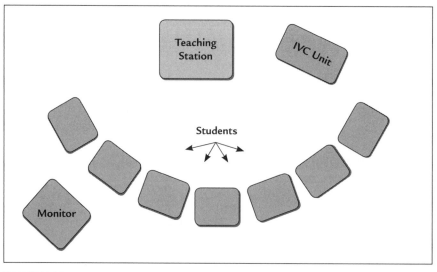

DIAGRAM 2

Some classrooms use tables rather than desks, as shown in Diagram 3. The work-group setup allows students to collaborate on projects easily and make group presentations while seated. Tables enable whole-group instruction or presentation and can be moved into a variety of configurations to support alternative learning activities. Remote and near-sites feel more connected because the room is easily configured to match the content and activities planned for the lesson. The IVC unit is located centrally to optimize camera pan and tilt functions. Wall-mounted monitors are adjustable, enabling optimal views for all participants.

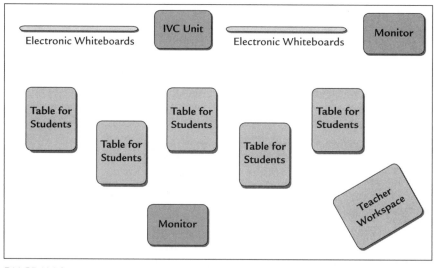

DIAGRAM 3

Note that each of these configurations has a teacher workspace. This is a key element and provides a place to integrate various teaching and display tools, such as the mouse and keyboard, control tablet, remote control, document camera, and other user interfaces.

Critical elements to consider when designing an IVC classroom include:

1. Visibility for all participants
2. Ability to reconfigure the classroom to meet a variety of instructional and collaborative needs (multipurpose use)
3. Interactivity with remote sites and on-site teacher or facilitator
4. Ability to use on-site supplemental media (VCRs, DVD player, computers, etc.)
5. Ability to support a variety of instructional strategies

Equipment

Numerous options are available for a videoconferencing system, from a single-monitor desktop unit to a multiple-monitor room-sized setup. In this book, we focus on room-sized systems, which are most advantageous for classroom instruction. Many choices are also available within that arena. Final purchasing decisions should be determined based on the projected use of the technology.

The following equipment checklist will help you with decision making and get you started in creating a list of purchases for your videoconferencing facility. Equipment vendors will be happy to assist you and your technology staff in making equipment choices; it's usually best to heed their advice because you'll probably have to live with your decisions for quite some time. Some examples of variables to keep in mind when making these decisions include: the size of your classroom or facility, the number of people who might use the facility at any given time, whether the room will be dedicated to IVC activities only or shared with other users for other purposes, how the system will be used by your entire school community, what upgrades are available for the system and desired by potential users, and how your school might be able to build upon its initial investment.

Equipment Checklist

✓ **Monitors (2).** The size of your monitors and the size of the classroom determine visibility for on-site students and teachers. For a classroom-sized system, monitors should be 27–32 inches and should be placed in the line of sight for both teacher and students.

✓ **Mobile cabinetry and carts.** Movable units, even within the classroom, provide a setting where participants can move around, change the classroom configuration to meet activity needs, and optimize their interaction with each other and with the far-site. Mobility helps make the equipment more manageable and user-friendly.

✓ **Camera.** Placement of the camera for optimal site-to-site interaction is critical. To facilitate eye contact, the primary camera should be placed above the primary monitor. As students gaze at the monitor, they also look directly into the camera, creating the illusion of eye contact and helping to reinforce the feeling of face-to-face communication. Without the appearance of eye contact, participants may quickly lose interest. On another note, if you are purchasing new equipment, be sure to budget for a high definition camera. Even at lower bandwidths, resolution is much improved over traditional cameras.

✓ **Presentation computer.** The addition of an external computer enhances the interactive media functions, access to the Internet, and use of the computer's program applications.

✓ **Document camera.** This camera provides an additional projection device for instructional purposes. Teachers should have easy access to this tool during the videoconference. A less expensive way to show documents and 3-D objects, or to add an extra camera source, is the flex cam.

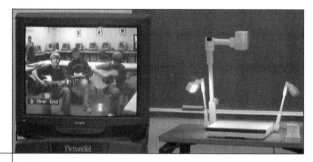

A document camera set up beside a monitor.

✓ **Microphones.** Microphone placement is critical and should be based on manufacturers' guidelines. Optimal audio functionality can make or break a videoconference. Microphones have ON/OFF settings that can be left open or configured for push-to-talk operation. It's imperative that microphones not be limited to an ON position. The resulting background noise caused by an open microphone will degrade a videoconference. Positioning of the microphone is also critical. Microphones positioned too close to the monitor will create a sound reverberation and can result in considerable frustration for participants. Remember, for a "fixed" IVC room, a ceiling-mounted microphone is ideal.

✓ **Remote control.** Manipulation of the IVC system and its ***external devices*** can be carried out by the remote control, enabling teachers to integrate external devices into their instructional presentation with the push of a button. This feature allows teachers or presenters extended mobility within the classroom so that they can walk away from the teacher station and still have control over system functions. It should be locked up when not in use and placed for easy access during a videoconference.

Equipment Support

Talk to your IT manager about the wisdom of purchasing an extended maintenance contract when you buy your IVC system. In some cases this can be a prudent decision, but in others it might be a costly and unnecessary additional expense. Many states or districts have people on the payroll who have been trained to make standard repairs on videoconferencing systems. In addition, it's frequently cheaper to replace a broken component than it is to maintain a costly annual extended contract.

For day-to-day assistance, you may have a districtwide technical support structure that allows you to call upon an established help desk for equipment or network problems. You may also, over time, learn how to troubleshoot first- or second-level problems with the equipment. Whatever support structure you have available to you, we recommend posting a troubleshooting guide, visible to all users of your IVC classroom, that includes on-site and off-site phone numbers, pager numbers, and, if possible, alternative phone numbers. It may also be helpful to post what the user should not do in the event of an emergency.

Useful Tips for IVC Classroom Configuration

Included below are additional items to consider adding to your shopping list as you design and equip your IVC classroom. We've also provided a few tips to help you establish a functional system and create a facility that will be user-friendly for everyone.

1. Install an outside phone line with long-distance connectivity so that your remote partners will have quick and easy access to you in case of problems, no matter what time of day or night it might be.

2. Install a fax machine, also connected to an outside line. This provides one more connectivity option should the IVC technology fail or it's after school hours and the front office is closed. The fax machine also offers an easy avenue for sharing documents and critical information during a videoconference.

3. Consider incorporating a laptop lab in the classroom. This provides students with an opportunity to work offline during the course of an IVC class or presentation.

4. Place basic user instructions at each seat and at the teacher podium/workstation.

5. Put operating instructions and other user guidelines in a binder and place it next to the IVC unit.

6. Provide a wall clock so that teachers/presenters can keep track of time and pace their presentation accordingly without looking down at their watch.

7. Turn off the school's intercom system in the IVC classroom.

8. Have someone in the building accessible by phone or beeper to assist with troubleshooting and basic equipment maintenance.

Staffing

Virtual learning programs, and especially IVC programs, require the expertise and support of several people. Because of limited school budgets, in many cases this support is carried out by one or two people wearing several IVC hats. We believe the following positions—whether staffed by one person or by a couple of multitasking support personnel—are crucial for the operation of a successful IVC program:

- Virtual learning facilitator
- Tech support specialist
- Program support staff
- Teacher of record

Virtual Learning Specialist

Many school systems are beginning to recognize the importance of funding a virtual learning specialist position. The person who fills this role often works at the district office or Service Center to identify, develop, and organize virtual learning opportunities for teachers and students.

Depending on the distance education mission of the organization and the amount of funding available, the day-to-day activities of virtual learning specialists may vary. They may supervise and expedite the delivery of IVC classes. They may be responsible for setting up and equipping classrooms, selecting and training teachers and facilitators, and ensuring the class runs smoothly on both the "send" and "receive" end.

In other situations, these specialists are also in charge of increasing the instructional technology skills of all teachers in the district. They may assist teachers in locating supplementary IVC content that highlights existing curriculum.

The virtual learning specialist may handle scheduling tasks for IVC events, depending on the size of the operation. As numbers of participating schools within the district increase, a specialist may be identified in each building to be on hand for consultation and troubleshooting.

Virtual learning specialists should have classroom teaching experience, knowledge of curriculum development, and at least fundamental understanding of distance delivery and interactive videoconferencing. They must be well organized and possess excellent people skills.

Virtual Learning Coordinator

In a classroom situation, virtual learning coordinators provide production support both prior to and during a videoconference. They operate the equipment and set up the room; they may function as a classroom aide or teaching partner. The coordinator works closely with the teacher, assisting with both classroom management and course delivery logistics. The coordinator may identify a responsible adult to facilitate the videoconference in either or both locations. For an ongoing class, it's imperative to have a facilitator at each remote site. The facilitator at each far-site becomes the eyes, ears, hands, and feet for teachers of record, arranging handouts and textbooks, turning in assignments, and reporting back to the teacher on any problems a student may be experiencing.

During a ***multipoint videoconference***, a facilitator can help coordinate many details, such as conducting ***test calls*** with each participating site, creating and confirming schedules, and assuring that all participants are on target. In most states, having a certified teacher in the classroom is the law. These states argue that only a certified teacher is able to determine if students are indeed on task and learning. There's also a liability concern when facilitators are not certified teachers; should students become injured or harmed during the class period, the school may not be covered. In some states, the person at the remote site must be a licensed teacher as well.

During a virtual field trip or specialized class or event provided by professional content providers, the facilitator role is more like that of a news anchor. Although plenty of behind-the-scenes activity occurs, in this situation the facilitator's main job is to move the videoconference along and ensure that both speaker and audience needs are met. During a multipoint videoconference, the facilitator cues presenter and students when to speak, acknowledges each site when it's the site participants' turn to interact, asks questions, and makes comments as appropriate. The facilitator may even encourage participation to ensure that enough interaction takes place. A facilitator may also assist the presenter with a demonstration, much like a teacher's aide, transitioning from one camera to another and helping make the presentation seamless and smooth. Unfortunately, because of budget and qualified staff constraints, teachers often have to serve as both presenter and facilitator.

Many states are now taking a fresh look at standards and practices that guide staffing in IVC classrooms. Because the need to access content from a distance may be based on lack of certified staff at the local site, requiring a licensed teacher at each far-site may not be practical in some situations and may even defeat the purpose of the IVC program.

Tech Support Specialist

Someone on-site trained to troubleshoot system problems, interface with the network hub, and solve minor equipment problems should never be more than a phone call away when the IVC system is in use. In a situation where users are new to the technology, the tech support specialist should be on hand to make sure the system is turned on, dialed in, and functioning properly. Microphone tests and camera tests should be conducted prior to the start of the conference. Nothing is more annoying or disruptive than troubleshooting that has to take place after the conference has begun. Tech support personnel can demonstrate to new users and guests how to operate the equipment, especially the push-to-talk microphones. We've seen situations where IVC guests were left alone without a clue about how to use the microphones, distressing the conference with open microphones or not being able to operate the microphones at all.

The result of inadequate tech support is often a failed videoconference, which places undue stress on the participants and typically leaves them very skeptical about the technology and eager to tell everyone that IVC is a waste of time.

Program Support Staff

An ongoing IVC class, like any academic program, requires staff and student support services. For an IVC class, where students and teachers are often separated by many miles, details such as the ones that follow need to be attended to on a regular basis:

- Distribution of papers, assignments, and handouts
- Interaction with the business office regarding tuition and grading issues
- Oversight of day-to-day logistics
- Textbook coordination
- Information dissemination
- First-level troubleshooting of equipment
- Arrangement for facilitator's backup

ARKANSAS GOES THE DISTANCE

Chris Robbins, Director of Outreach; Arkansas School for Mathematics, Sciences, and the Arts; University of Arkansas System; Hot Springs, Arkansas

Five years ago, Horatio High School (Horatio, Arkansas) principal James Dobbins was in a difficult position. Unable to hire a certified Spanish instructor after months of searching, it appeared the school couldn't offer Spanish courses to its students, potentially costing them college scholarship opportunities and even admission to some colleges and universities.

Faced with this possibility, Dobbins decided to explore distance education, an educational method he'd used to complete coursework as a graduate student. For assistance, Dobbins turned to the Office of Distance Education at the Arkansas School for Mathematics, Sciences, and the Arts. Five years later he still raves about ODE and the service it provides the students of Horatio.

"It's just been spectacular," Dobbins says. "I told the principal over at Lafayette County High School (Stamps, Arkansas) recently how great it's been for us."

Curtis Black, a softball and girls basketball coach at Horatio who's been the school's facilitator, agrees, although when Black first heard about using distance education to teach students, he wasn't sure how it would work.

"When we started out, I was skeptical the kids wouldn't learn as much or as well," Black says. "I didn't know how well the students would respond with the teacher not being in the classroom with them. But after a month or so, I could tell it was going to work for us. It's a great thing."

To accomplish these tasks most effectively, it's important for near-sites and far-sites to communicate on a daily basis. E-mail attachments provide an efficient way to transfer documents, samples, and handouts to remote sites, with the facilitator making copies at that location. Establishing a conference website may also benefit students, allowing them easy access to files and media presented in class. Sharing e-mail addresses or setting up an e-mail list can further enhance information flow between sites. A central processor should collect fees and ensure that all students know which materials are required for the course. In some cases, IVC rooms have designated technicians to check lines and equipment before any connection. These technicians may substitute as the designated facilitator if necessary.

Teacher of Record

The *teacher of record* is the most crucial participant in a successful virtual learning program, often wearing many—or even all—of the staff "hats" outlined above. Whether the videoconference is an ongoing class or a virtual field trip involving an off-site content provider, the teacher plays a pivotal role in organizing and mediating the program.

Teaching and learning from a distance is not intuitive. Expect to spend extra time preparing for a videoconference class or event. Important aspects of the IVC teacher's role are the additional and special arrangements that must be made ahead of time, weaving particular instructional and administrative elements into the lesson plan (see Chapter 4). Since most teachers are relatively new to this technology, we recommend at least some level of training and practice prior to an IVC event or the launch of a daily IVC class. Finally, if classroom students are also new to the medium, the teacher should take plenty of time to instruct students about the logistics, protocol, and etiquette of participating in a video-conference (see Chapter 5).

Natalie Humphreys, Arkansas Office of Distance Education's Spanish instructor and 2007 USDLA Bronze Award winner, reviews with her Spanish II students at Turrell High School before they begin taking a quiz.

Training

Teaching with videoconferencing technologies requires new skills and an ability to adapt to new ways of teaching and communicating. Teachers who are given an opportunity to train and practice will be successful and will continue to use the technology. The cost of this training is minimal, sometimes free, and can be accomplished very efficiently if well planned ahead of time. Technology staff should also receive training from equipment vendors and state-level videoconferencing specialists. Many vendors are happy to bring technology staff up to speed at no charge.

Take a moment to recall the hours of training and practice you've spent integrating computer technologies into your classroom. Many preservice teacher training programs are now rich with technology integration, most often in the form of online learning. For example, in 2005 7% of all U.S. postsecondary students were participating in an online course (Mendenhall, 2007). This, matched with the increase in availability of videoconference technology, provides teachers the opportunity to become more familiar with not only the technology but also the experience of distance learning.

Stories abound about high-end, high-priced IVC equipment sitting unused in corners and closets—and sometimes still in boxes—because of lack of training for both teachers and technology staff.

Teachers who participate in some form of distance learning are more likely to recognize the significance of global classrooms. Transitioning from a traditional face-to-face classroom situation to a distance classroom situation is an ongoing learning process. Professional development should be ongoing and in-depth.

IVC training programs should address a variety of topics and should be offered to teachers through various resources. Critical training themes, in addition to basic operation of the technology, should address instructional design, video production, graphics production, presentation strategies, logistics, protocol, and classroom management. We'll address these issues in detail in Chapter 5, but we encourage all new users to access an interactive training program from an experienced educational videoconference practitioner.

Oregon teachers are using IVC to form a virtual learning community supported by a blend of other communications technologies. Here, they're connected to the Oregon Museum of Science and Industry.

Eliminating the Initial Fear Factor

Once a videoconference system is correctly installed, it's easy to learn how to use the basic controls, applications, and peripherals. Systems are often operated with a simple touch-pad or remote control. We encourage new users to employ a seat-of-the-pants method to familiarize themselves with the equipment. Take the controls in hand and practice manipulating the camera, microphone, monitor, and so forth. Like a desktop computer, these systems are fairly robust, and it's not likely you'll break anything by experimenting with the menus and controls. If you're already proficient with a desktop computer system and a TV remote control, you will probably find IVC technology to be fairly intuitive. Practice makes perfect!

TEACHER OBSERVATIONS USING IVC

Donna M. Farren, M.Ed., Distance Learning Specialist
Monroe 2-Orleans BOCES; Rochester, New York

Our organization uses videoconferencing as part of the staff development program for teachers in the reading program. Each teacher who participates in the program has to teach a student lesson while the rest of the teachers observe. In the past, the students were transported to our location, and the teachers observed the lesson behind a one-way mirror. Transporting the students was complicated, and some of the teachers participating in the program worked at schools an hour or more away.

Now we use videoconferencing; so the teacher teaches the students in his or her home classroom and the rest of the teachers observe via videoconference. Originally, we thought we were only eliminating transportation issues, but we found other benefits as well. The students remain in their regular classroom; so it is a more natural environment for observation. It also helps with last- minute cancellations when a student is sick; the teacher can select a different student. It also exposes a lot of new teachers to videoconferencing.

After teachers and technology staff have mastered the rudiments of the technology, many things must be considered before incorporating IVC for instructional purposes. While we discuss many of these issues in Chapter 5, there's no substitute for hands-on practice. In a training or practice situation, teachers can divide up in off-site groups, brainstorm possible applications, generate lesson plans, and present to each other from a distance, utilizing various elements and applications of the system. This is an opportunity to offer honest feedback and share knowledge, frustrations, and "Aha!" moments of enlightenment. Another way to generate honest feedback is to tape your own presentation and share it with colleagues.

Taking the Next Step

The next step in your IVC training program should be to survey an array of possible applications and pedagogical techniques. Seek out examples of IVC applications in K–12 classrooms wherever you can find them. Some programs provide web-based ***archived video streams*** of past IVC events. The Northwest Educational Technology Center (NETC) Digital Bridges project, for example, offers website examples and two videos filled with excellent illustrations and IVC guidelines.

We recommend a formal faculty or staff training program of up to 24 hours. The workshop might be broken up into half-day increments and extended over several weeks. We also recommend that you follow up any training program with ongoing practice and actual participation.

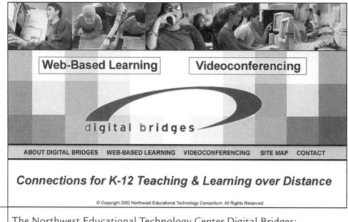

The Northwest Educational Technology Center Digital Bridges:
www.netc.org/digitalbridges

IVC Training Opportunities

IVC training sessions are often offered at the district level, especially if there's been an investment in the technology by the school system. In many states, local education associations and service centers provide training and support in the adoption of virtual learning technologies. In some cases, training is available on the state level and is offered through the state Department of Education. Vendors of the videoconference equipment may also offer training in the use of IVC in the classroom. We suggest you check the virtual learning (distance education) websites of all of these organizations for resources and support program opportunities.

> **KEY TO SUCCESS**
>
> Support and incentives offered by school administrators are a key factor for your success as an IVC teacher or practitioner.

If you don't have access to an established training program through your local or state education system, other options are available. More and more state and national technology conferences offer workshops, or at least a concurrent session, on the topic. ISTE's NECC hosts several IVC-focused sessions and workshops. If you can attend one of these conferences, these are also good places to network with like-minded professionals and potential partners.

Professional content providers may also provide staff development opportunities. For example, the Cleveland (Ohio) Museum of Art offers middle and high school teachers a program called Professional Development: DL and Your Curriculum.

The course curriculum includes an introduction to videoconferencing and Internet resources, a lesson on how to integrate these resources into classroom projects, and a culminating videoconference with the museum.

Professional Development: DL and Your Curriculum program at the Cleveland
Museum of Art: www.clemusart.com/educef/distance/7126785.aspx

Numerous virtual learning organizations offer training materials online. Their websites
provide downloadable PDF files containing technical information, content access information, and tips on how to plan your own videoconference or IVC workshop. Nassau BOCES
in New York state offers free to all teachers an online self-paced course called Introduction
to Videoconferencing.

Nassau BOCES: www.nassauboces.org/cit/vls/selfpaced.htm

DID YOU KNOW?

Within ISTE there are two special interest groups devoted to distance learning.

• SIGIVC promotes understanding of interactive videoconferencing and related virtual learning technologies within the K–12 education community by advancing collaboration, information dissemination, research, and practices.

• SIGTel is a network of educators involved with computer-based communications—either standalone stations or combined with other media. The SIGTel Bulletin reflects the SIG's interests and activities in the areas of communications, projects, research, publications, international connections, and training.

To find out more, visit www.iste.org and click on Membership, Special Interest Groups.

Many educators also take advantage of the ATT Knowledge Network Explorer website. Founded in 1992, they offer valuable free information and assistance on instructional strategies, multipoint videoconferencing, IVC equipment strategies, IVC communication skills, planning a videoconference, evaluating a videoconference, and more.

E-mail lists and electronic bulletin boards also support K–12 videoconferencing and engage a variety of people from the field, including content providers, end users, teachers, researchers, and product vendors. E-mail lists provide daily opportunities to access ideas, opportunities, and tips on advancing or streamlining a local IVC program (for a selection of best e-mail lists, see Chapter 7).

We believe the importance of training and practice for successful integration of IVC technologies cannot be overstated. Successful distance delivery requires as much or more advanced planning, organization, and training as preparation for face-to-face classes. But you may not have to drive hundreds of miles to access the training workshop or practice with your peers; these opportunities are only as far away as your computer or IVC unit. You need only make the necessary arrangements and schedule the time to do it.

Chapter 4

Planning a Videoconference

The supplemental IVC event and the daily IVC class are the two primary types of instructional videoconference. A supplemental IVC event usually occurs just once and is intended to enrich or enhance existing curriculum. The daily IVC class or program, on the other hand, is presented on a regular basis over an extended period of time. The specific planning activities and logistical support you'll need for either kind of IVC will depend largely on whether you're delivering content or receiving it—or both. However, in all instances, careful coordination with all participants is always necessary. Though a variety of people (or roles) might be involved in the implementation of a videoconference, the focus of this chapter is on the preplanning activities that teachers, virtual learning coordinators, and students should undertake before the cameras and microphones are turned on.

Preplanning for a Supplemental IVC

You can supplement your curriculum numerous ways through the use of IVC in the classroom. We'll focus here on the planning and logistical coordination that should go into a curriculum enrichment or enhancement program. Enrichment programs are available through professional content providers and often take the form of a virtual field trip.

Curriculum Enrichment Videoconferences

To ensure a successful learning experience, numerous factors must be taken into account when preplanning and coordinating an enrichment videoconference. You should make sure the following occurs when considering this kind of supplemental videoconference:

- Content matches curriculum and grade level

- Content provider is reliable and responsive

- Program time and format match student availability

- Access to IVC equipment, facilities, and network bandwidth is adequate for the program format

- Students and teachers are adequately prepared

- Support personnel are available and prepared

PREPLANNING FOR TEACHERS

Preplanning for a videoconference can help ensure content delivered is relevant and advantageous for students. For maximum effectiveness, videoconferences should be integrated into unit or daily lesson plans so that the virtual field trip fits your curriculum seamlessly. This takes careful planning. We advise that you prepare for the event a minimum of two weeks in advance to ensure an effective and beneficial encounter with a professional content provider.

The best time to begin planning a supplemental IVC activity is at the beginning of the school year or term. Once you know where to access resources (see Chapter 7), use your curriculum planning time to review content provider offerings and match them to your yearlong or term-long plans. Starting your planning well ahead of time will help you weigh both curricular and budgetary considerations. Since hundreds of providers offer programs on thousands of topics at a variety of costs, it's reasonable to expect to spend at least half a day reviewing potential matches for your classroom curriculum. Greenberg and Colbert (2002) itemize the following "Signs of Spectacular Content and Content Providers" (p. 12):

- Providers who lay it all out for educators, making it easy to access their instructional aids

- Programs that encourage students to work and not be passive recipients of the content delivery (pre-IVC activities for students will ensure a more focused event)

- Providers who are clear about the degree of interactivity to expect during the session

- Programs that integrate specific activities suited to the topic and designed for students to complete during the session

- Providers who have subject matter experts on hand or specific content programs applicable to your curriculum, and the ability to deliver them effectively

- Providers who incorporate a feedback mechanism—and who utilize the feedback to maximize quality

- Providers whose services include both technology and a human touch to run their program

- Providers who offer a blend of technical staff and educators

The more a program or content provider exhibits these qualities, the more likely it is that the experience will be high powered, high impact, and engagingly interactive for students.

OREGON CLASSROOM TAKES VIRTUAL FIELD TRIP: CARNEGIE MUSEUM OF NATURAL HISTORY

Tammy Giffis, Teacher
Evergreen Elementary School; Cave Junction, Oregon

For my fifth grade class's first virtual field trip, we visited the Carnegie Museum of Natural History to study owls. After downloading information about owls from the museum, I divided the material into smaller sections for my students. Topics included myths and legends, and About Owls, parts 1 and 2. I invited the third grade TAG students to share the experience.

In preparation, the day before the virtual field trip we practiced connecting to another classroom. We had technical difficulties and couldn't see the other class, but we were still able to practice asking questions and sharing what we knew already about owls. Students practiced speaking and rotating the preset camera. As a culminating activity, students dissected owl pellets and graphed the results. Though technical obstacles cropped up, they were resolved through collaborative problem solving and patience.

Virtual field trips have opened up the world to my students and enhanced my teaching. I've learned the value of creating lessons that lead up to the virtual field trip and culminating lessons that follow. Being able to plan units of study centered around a virtual field trip, and having funds available for supplies that support those lessons, have made all of the troubleshooting worthwhile.

Professional development is also crucial for the success of the virtual field trip. We held three trainings this year, and the practice and research was invaluable.

Arkansas Office of Distance Education's French instructor Frances vandenHeuvel presents vocabulary while students at Huntsville High School, Parkers Chapel High School, and Northern Potter High School listen and read aloud.

PREPLANNING FOR STUDENTS

One of the most critical components of preplanning for an enrichment videoconference event is preparing students for the experience. It's crucial that the IVC content be interwoven into the natural flow of instruction and that students have the conceptual grounding necessary to engage actively in the presentation. For example, if the program features a researcher who specializes in medieval architecture, it would be prudent for students to have previously studied some of the major historical events of the Middle Ages and viewed pictures of the major styles of architecture from that time period. In some cases, it's possible for teachers to e-mail to the content provider in advance a short list of items pertinent to their curriculum so that the provider is aware of the class's special interests.

Enrichment IVC may not always include a content provider. Teachers may determine that skills can best be reinforced by having students present directly to peers. In this case, teachers at both near and remote sites can collaboratively plan lessons that will involve having their students work in teams and present to the other site. The best-case scenario would be for one or more students from the near-site to partner with one or more students at the remote site. These teams could work through e-mail, instant messaging, or a project website—or all three—prior to the videoconference, and all groups would virtually share, during the videoconference, the results of their collaboration. websites, wikispaces, and blogs are some tools that may be used to extend the lesson beyond the videoconference.

FORMAT CONSIDERATIONS

Preplanning activities should include learning about the policies, procedures, and format of the content provider or virtual field trip you are considering. Pachnowski (2002) suggests that the following items be confirmed prior to scheduling a videoconference:

- The length of the videoconference, and day/time restrictions
- The cost to you (your school)

- The provider's policy should the event fail to "connect"

- The amount of interactivity available to students during the IVC

- The hands-on materials available to students for use before, during, or after the IVC

- The equipment and network bandwidth necessary to take full advantage of the program

It's also advisable to determine if the videoconference addresses local, state, or national content standards. This information will help you enlist much-needed administrative support for incorporating the IVC into your regular learning activities. Professional content providers should list this information as part of their content descriptions. Connecting standards with activities is a must for today's teachers. Identifying this information ahead of time makes it much easier for teachers to recognize and use available resources. Teachers who are able to connect a concept or skill standard to a particular activity and then to outside resources (virtual or otherwise) are at a great advantage.

Curriculum Enhancement Videoconferences

If no professional content provider has a ready-made program that adequately serves your needs, you can always try to create a program on your own or in collaboration with like-minded colleagues. Classroom partnerships, school-to-work activities, cultural exchanges, and guest speakers are a few of the supplemental IVCs you can arrange on your own, employing your ingenuity, creativity, and coordination skills to build a customized enhancement program. With this kind of IVC, you may function as the receiving teacher, the delivery teacher, or a combination of both. We suggest that teachers and virtual learning specialists prepare to play a dynamic role in these videoconferences by addressing the following in their preplanning activities:

- What technology will be used

- What curriculum materials will be needed

- What facilities will be required

- What learning styles will be addressed and which teaching methods will be employed

- How content will be integrated into existing curriculum

TECHNOLOGY PLANNING

Your system should be set up, tested, and ready to go. It's usually disastrous if you have to troubleshoot the system either at the beginning of a videoconference or during it; so make sure beforehand that the equipment works and you know how to operate it. Work with your on-site technician to ensure the equipment is capable of providing quality voice and video. You or the technician should conduct a test call prior to the videoconference. If problems arise with the technology during the IVC, have a backup plan in place. While it's unlikely that your videoconference will be a total disaster, it's wise to have an alternate activity ready for the students, just in case. If your audio or video equipment malfunctions, you'll need to decide whether to disconnect or make adaptations.

STUDENTS PREPARED TO USE EQUIPMENT

Bill Dynes, Professor; University of Indianapolis; Indianapolis, Indiana

One concern that faculty have about videoconferencing is that the technology will exacerbate the psychological distance separating students and instructors. That anxiety was put to rest for me one day when I was teaching an IVC composition class linking students at three remote sites with our campus. Early in the semester, the students were still fairly shy. One class began with a fortuitous glitch: our site could see and hear each of the remote sites, and each of the remote sites could see and hear one another, but none of them had any contact with us. So they didn't know they were still under supervision. I half expected them to abandon class and half dreaded what I'd overhear them saying about their instructor. To my surprise, they switched on the document cameras in their rooms and launched into a rousing game of Hangman! By the time full connectivity was restored, I'd seen solid evidence both that my students could in fact interact with each other comfortably using IVC and that they could use the equipment in creative ways.

MATERIALS PLANNING

Work closely with all participants (students, teachers, guest speakers) to ensure that the needed materials are provided to everyone prior to the actual videoconference(s). If you're working with a content provider, you may have been sent preliminary materials for the students to cover before the videoconference, or to use during the videoconference. Make sure you have enough copies for all students. If the lesson is a hands-on experience, have all necessary supplies ready before the IVC.

NAME CARDS

Have students make name cards that identify their project, as well as site signs to identify their location if more than one site is involved.

FACILITIES PLANNING

If the IVC technology in your school isn't located in your classroom, we suggest that before you prepare yourself and your students for the IVC event, you check with your technology staff or support staff, or your technology facilitator, to make certain the facilities and technology are available that day and will meet your needs. In some cases, you may have to make arrangements to transport your students to another location in your district to gain access. With today's viability of mobile and desktop units, this scenario is less frequently the case. Whatever your situation, the goal is to have students prepared and in the right place at the right time for the videoconference. If you must move students to another location outside your classroom, plan on arriving early to situate and prepare your students prior to the start of the videoconference.

METHODOLOGY PLANNING

Interactive videoconferencing is a teaching tool that supports ***constructivist instructional theories.*** Through practice, you'll learn to integrate and revise your teaching methodologies to take the best advantage of this tool. As the teacher, you'll be able to direct your students' learning experience so that they'll be able to synthesize project-based content with past and future learning. The interweaving of the IVC event into the flow of student learning is a key element for success.

Project-based learning (PBL) allows students the freedom to connect with one another on many levels, with a tangible product as the end result. However, the outcome and true value of PBL comprises more than just the end product. By working together, students learn how to communicate more effectively with peers, how to share ideas and elaborate on their feelings, how to defend their actions and ideals, and how to respect others. When a virtual dimension is part of the PBL experience, students gain an even greater understanding of their place in the world. They have a deeper understanding of time and space and can conceptualize in a much more substantial way when they see and hear in real time through IVC. The IVC event alone can be constructive in nature when students lead the learning.

High schools embracing Big Picture School and Small Learning Community models would greatly benefit from the use of IVC. Advisor and advisee meetings could be held via videoconference outside of regular school hours, and students could build relationships with peers by learning the appropriate way to interact in a virtual environment. Career and technical programs could be explored in ways not previously imagined. For instance, high school students interested in a construction career could collaborate with a construction company via videoconference and actually view construction sites and converse with the site supervisor. Students could take responsibility for setting up videoconferences as a class project. The level of interaction a high school student could have within an IVC project could be significantly greater than that of an elementary, or even middle school, student.

CONTENT INTEGRATION

Plan IVC lessons to match the sequence of your regular instruction, preparing students ahead of time for the IVC content by working on related projects. For example, students can prepare science projects or research findings and present them to a content expert. The expert can then provide face-to-face feedback on their work, giving the lesson a compelling twist.

Like traditional instruction, IVC lessons should have objectives, activities, and assessment components. Your lesson preplans should focus on what you want your students to learn from the experience as well as how technology will support that learning. Tell students ahead of time what the goal is. Evaluation, as always, should directly reflect the measurable objective.

TEXAS INSPIRATION: STUDENTS AS CONTENT PROVIDERS!

Tommy Bearden, Distance Learning Consultant
Region 14 Education Service Center; Abilene, Texas

Tommy Bearden inspires students to become "the teacher" by creating and presenting information to others around the world using interactive videoconferencing. Tommy helped a local high school implement the virtual field trip titled Cotton: Plant of Many Uses, in which students from across the United States and Europe were able to learn about cotton from their peers at Stamford High School (Stamford, Texas). Not only did the students prepare the content, conduct the presentation, and support the equipment, but they also mailed cotton bolls and other manipulatives in advance so that students could have a hands-on experience.

Tommy believes students can deliver content simply by looking in their backyards. He has sponsored several student-driven events, such as A Walk Along the Brazos River, Our State—A Brief History and Fun Facts, and a collaborative event about the Civil War in which students presented on their state's impact on the war. With these events, students were encouraged to use multimedia resources to present their content. In A Walk Along the Brazos River, students took video cameras to the river and embedded recorded video throughout their PowerPoint presentations.

Last year Tommy coordinated 230 field trips that more than 11,000 students in his region either participated in or viewed. While most of those field trips were not student created, Tommy understands the value videoconferencing brings into the classroom in terms of fostering new skills and making learning real. Within every student who participates in IVC presentations and becomes accustomed to learning through IVC lies a potential "teacher."

Preplanning for Daily IVC Classes

If you're a teacher or a virtual classroom coordinator who will regularly support K–12 students as they receive curriculum content and instruction from a distance, many of your planning and preparation activities will be the same as those listed above for the one-time, or short duration, supplemental IVC. However, a few additional considerations should be kept in mind when you're planning to receive a daily IVC class:

1. **Review the class syllabus, making sure it meets students' needs:**

    * Does the curriculum meet established instructional standards in your state or district?

- Does the content match a class sequence (e.g., Spanish II or III, World History I or II)?

- If the class is designated Advanced Placement, what qualifies the curriculum content as an AP strand?

- Does the content repeat or duplicate what your students have completed in the past?

- Do you have special-needs students, and will their needs be met?

> **PARTNERSHIP PLANNING**
>
> Plan for daily IVC classes in partnership with delivery teachers and facilitators.

2. **Check class times and student availability:**

   - Are there any bell-schedule conflicts (one of the most common problems for daily IVC classes)?

   - If so, can students and school administrators overcome the conflict through a more flexible scheduling plan?

3. **Confirm costs for the class:**

   - Will there be a cost to the district for the class?

   - If there's a fee (many public school providers need to recoup the cost of providing the IVC class), will the district pay?

   - If the cost is high, can neighboring districts trade IVC classes to share that cost?

   - Are there any district policies regarding in-district and out-of-district students, and who must pay to participate in a class?

4. **Find out what materials (including textbooks) are required:**

   - Will students be adequately prepared to participate from Day One of the IVC class?

   - If textbooks are required, will your district pay for them?

   - If students need other materials (e.g., lab supplies, art supplies, math tools), who will be responsible for supplying them, and will the district pay for them?

5. **Allot a period of time to familiarize students with the technology:**

   - Schedule time to familiarize students with the technology prior to the first day of the IVC class.

   - Coordinate this activity with the remote teacher (teacher of record), if possible.

6. **Prepare yourself to use and support the IVC technology:**

   - Know ahead of time what might go wrong with the technology and some of the basic troubleshooting strategies you will need to employ.

   - Plan ahead with the remote teacher how the teacher will proceed if there's a technology failure.

   - Familiarize yourself with the interactive features of the IVC system and how you can maximize them for student use.

7. **Check into the reliability of the remote teacher and program:**

   - If you're importing a class from out of district or out of state, know who you're dealing with.

   - Meet with the program's administrators prior to signing your students up for the class and resolve any potential conflicts.

8. **Clarify who will issue the grade and credit for the class:**

   - In many cases, the home school will accept the grade from the remote teacher and directly issue the credit from the home school, keeping administrative confusion to a minimum.

   - In some states, integrated data systems are being developed that will follow students wherever they access a class credit—from their home school, through an IVC class, or through an online, web-based class.

9. **Confer with your school administration regarding financial arrangements:**

   - Make sure agreements on costs and payments are in place before the class begins.

   - In some cases, parents may be asked to pay for the class; if so, a payment schedule should be established in writing ahead of time.

10. **Arrange for technical support:**

    - The on-site teacher or classroom facilitator should expect to handle first- and second-level technology issues.

    - If problems exceed this level, it's critical that higher-level technical support personnel are on hand, either in the building or accessible by phone, to solve any major issues that may arise.

    - Technical-support personnel should be part of the planning and setup process for the class. Use instant messaging as a technical support tool.

11. **Exchange staff contact information:**

    - All participating sites and personnel should have contact information on hand and easily accessible for everyone involved (class teachers, facilitators, on-site technical support, and network managers).

    - A laminated emergency call sheet should be posted next to your IVC unit.

12. **Provide the teacher of record with pertinent information about participating students:**

    - Communicate critical information about each student: special needs they may have, bad days, learning styles, tendencies, and so forth.

    - If you see a student having trouble during the class, communicate that information to the remote teacher as best you can.

Preplanning with school personnel, the remote teacher, program administrators, and the participating students is critical to success and will help ensure that the normal chaos factor doesn't unduly interfere with teaching and learning from a distance once the program is launched.

ELEMENTARY SCHOOL TRAVELS THE WORLD

Judith Dallinger, Library Media Specialist
Jack C. Binion Elementary; Richland Hills, Texas

Distance learning is an important part of the elementary curriculum in the Birdville Independent School District. This North Central Texas district is located in the suburban Fort Worth area. It provides curriculum-related IVC connections for all first- and third-grade students.

During the holiday season the personnel from the district technology and information management systems office provide a connection to the North Pole for all first-grade students. Students write a letter to Santa asking him for only one thing and persuading him through their letters that they deserve this gift. On the day of the connection, Santa, Mrs. Claus, and their head elf meet the students. Santa selects random letters to read and questions the students who wrote those letters. Everyone sings songs together, then Santa goes through his lists to discover which list each student's name appears on. (Of course, all students are on the good list!)

In another project, the district science consultant, posing as Solar Max, takes all of the third-grade students on a tour of the solar system. Students research the planets in the solar system before the connection and use the clues that Max provides to determine the mystery planet destination. Props such as fans and masks are provided as "protective" gear to the students.

The third-grade classes that have read *Stone Fox,* a book about a boy who trains for and competes in a dog sled race in Wyoming, connect to mushers preparing for the Iditarod race in Alaska.

Many fourth-grade students in the district connect to share descriptive writing and review for state tests via a distance learning *Jeopardy*-type game.

Our students are required to know the difference between urban, suburban, and rural schools. The most ambitious projects at Watauga Elementary School (Watauga, Texas) in the 2006–2007 school year were connections between urban and rural schools. Many students don't understand what life is like in a rural area. Using a three-way connection, we were able to connect students in schools in New York City with students in rural areas around the country, including one school in Alaska. Students submitted questions, and students from the various communities answered these student-generated questions.

Future plans include connecting to an elementary school in Louisiana to allow that school to present information to our students about Mardi Gras and share mascots. Connections with schools in New York are also planned, to study the various types of weather encountered in Texas and New York. Blogs and wikis will be a part of these connections.

Our funds are limited; so local site managers design many of our connections. Using e-mail lists and websites, these managers post requests to collaborate.

Preplanning for Teaching an IVC Class

In the preceding sections we outlined steps teachers should take to prepare themselves, their students, and their IVC classrooms to participate as end users of a supplemental IVC event or a daily IVC class. In this section, we'll outline preplanning requirements for the delivery of these same types of IVC classes and programs.

Delivering instruction from a distance requires new teaching skills. This skill set includes both performance elements (e.g., voice timbre and cadence, control of gesture, and eye contact) and technical elements—in other words, knowing how to prepare all the necessary components of a successful IVC class. If you're doing this for the first time, keep in mind that if you plan ahead and work closely with everyone who will be involved, from the technology staff to the teachers or facilitators at each remote site, you and your students will reap the benefits later.

Portions of planning an IVC class or collaborative project are like planning an in-house event. You plan ahead to make sure everyone's needs are addressed, information has been disseminated, rooms have been reserved, the right people have been invited, the technology is in place, and, if necessary, the event has been marketed and promoted. In addition to these critical logistical details, your lesson plan should be designed to support the unique instructional requirements of an IVC class. Following are some tips and ideas to guide you in preparing to teach an IVC class or deliver or facilitate a collaborative IVC program or project.

Technology Planning

Know the strengths and weaknesses of your technology. Know how to use all the equipment effectively and get any necessary training and practice ahead of time. Make sure your technology support system and staff are in place and will be on hand during class time, should you need them.

It will probably be up to you to arrange for and justify the expense of additional supporting technologies such as outside phone lines, fax machines, VCRs, and so forth. Start this process as early as possible because these requests may have to filter through the chain of command at your school or district.

Materials Planning

Your instructional goals will guide even your preplanning activities. Create a script for each presentation or class and incorporate it into the lesson plan (see Chapter 5 for a sample lesson plan and script). Use the script as a preplanning guide for instructional materials and media development. If you have a website that supports your class, you can use the site to post materials needed, requirements, a brief overview of the class, and your backup plan. It's also a good idea to begin any IVC class with a set of graphic guidelines you can display using a timed PowerPoint presentation. Graphics and presentation materials should be carefully designed (see Chapter 5 for some helpful guidelines). The slide below is an example of one that might precede an IVC program.

```
VIDEOCONFERENCE
REMINDERS

• Keep your microphone muted
  except when talking.

• Talk in a clear voice.

• Raise your hand to speak.
```

Instructional Planning for an IVC Class or Project

In Chapter 5 we'll outline in detail how to design and present an effective IVC class. For now, keep the following elements in mind as you begin to formulate the design of your class:

- The class should encourage student interaction.

- Instructional materials should be designed specifically for IVC use.

- Your instructional goals should be clear to everyone involved.

- Project-based, hands-on activities should be an overriding element of your class.

- Your communication skills should contribute to your ability to teach from a distance.

- Because you won't have the eye-to-eye vantage point from which to garner clues about whether students understand or are listening to your directions, you'll have to work extra hard to make a connection and drive your points home.

- Your body language will be a key communication tool and should be slightly exaggerated and purposeful.

- Back up these visual clues with extra written directions using the document camera, e-mail, and supporting websites.

Scheduling

Scheduling a videoconference includes several elements. Teachers must be sure to:

- Schedule the involvement of all participants (class registration).

- Schedule the use of all participating IVC sites (site confirmation).

- Schedule the use of the IVC network (network scheduling).

Primary scheduling activities are usually conducted by the delivery site. Though participating sites should reserve the use of their local facility, hosts of the videoconference

CONFIRM SCHEDULES

Your class is not completely scheduled until network and facilities scheduling has been confirmed by your network hub and the IVC schedulers of all participating sites.

(or their IVC scheduling staff) will be responsible for network scheduling, hosting the videoconference (if it is a multipoint conference) through their local network hub.

Prior to registration for the class or the virtual field trip, all sites should confirm the availability of their local IVC sites and network. Once this availability is confirmed, the host site will reserve and schedule the use of their network and arrange participation of all the far-sites. IP numbers, as well as contact information for support personnel, will be required before the scheduling process can take place (see Appendix A).

In the case of an ongoing class, scheduling activities should be completed well in advance to ensure network, technology, and facility availability. This is often accomplished prior to the end of the previous school year, shortly following class forecasting activities, but you can also make arrangements as opportunities arise.

Coordination and Logistics

The devil is always in the details. Coordinating an IVC, whether it's a one-time supplemental event or a daily class, involves several critical steps that must be taken in turn.

At first, keeping track of all these details will seem daunting. However, if your support systems are in place and you follow a step-by-step procedural guide, you'll be successful and everyone will benefit from, and even enjoy, the experience.

Work closely with everyone involved, keeping them informed along the way. If you're delivering a daily class or a supplemental event, provide student participants and their on-site facilitators with a packet of information that includes:

- Instructional information
- Site facilitator information
- Student support services information (website addresses, etc.)
- Additional resource information
- List of student expectations
- List of on-site facilitator expectations
- Disciplinary procedures
- Class syllabus and school calendar

Prior to the IVC event or class, be sure to:

- Send to remote sites handouts, book lists, and supply list.
- Make sure students have all necessary supplies in hand.

- Provide contact information to IVC staff (phone, fax, e-mail, etc.).
- Have contingency plans in place.
- Check time zones for each participating site.
- Pretest videoconference connections.
- Check classroom setup.
- Send out final confirmation notices or request confirmation from the content provider.
- Distribute and review IVC protocol and etiquette with your students.
- Prepare name and location signs.

If you are prepared, your students are prepared, the technology is ready, and all support staff are scheduled to be on hand, your IVC experience will infuse your classroom with excitement and a widening worldview for everyone involved. Remember, though, that videoconferencing equipment and systems are technology, not magic. When things go wrong—and you should not expect perfection, even with meticulous planning—try to keep a positive spin on the situation. Then, resort to your backup plan!

Evaluation

It's prudent to provide feedback to administrators, parents, and the rest of your education community so that they understand the significance of integrating videoconferencing into the instructional program at your school or district. You'll prevail if you develop an evaluation plan that addresses the quality of the technology, the delivery of content, and student transfer.

Whether you're a regular IVC user or a one-time experimenter, approach the evaluation process with both formative and summative strategies. For ongoing users, reflect upon the significant differences in student participation, the reliability of the technology, and the transfer of knowledge from the IVC lesson to instructional unit concepts. Recognizing the greater impact of these experiences upon your students requires a summative evaluation process where both formal and informal measures are taken.

EFFECTIVE EVALUATIONS

Both formal and informal evaluations are effective and acceptable.

You may choose to give pretests and posttests to determine what students gained from the experience. However, you are not limited to formal evaluations such as quizzes, skill tests, or a standardized test to measure the effectiveness of the instruction. In fact, formal evaluation procedures may not be the most productive forms of evaluating IVC integration. Some informal evaluation strategies are just as resourceful and provide immediate response to teacher and students. A sampling of informal evaluation tools include, but are not limited to:

- Observations collected during the videoconference to determine interactivity
- Journal writing
- Interactive student surveys (post-IVC)
- Sharing of survey results
- Review of student notes
- Class presentations

After participating in an IVC lesson, students will benefit from a short debriefing, providing time for students to reflect and for teachers to observe the learning process that may or may not have occurred.

You might want to keep a technology log to provide yourself and others with an overall assessment of the reliability of the system. Each time you connect a test call or an actual IVC, make a note in your log about quality and reliability. Include any troubleshooting steps that were required to resolve the issue. These records will also help when requesting technical assistance for IVC projects and will facilitate the maintenance of equipment and infrastructure so that they will always be in good running order and updated as needed.

SUGGESTION SESSION

Solicit student suggestions for future interactive videoconference activities.

Students should also be encouraged to assess the value that IVC adds to their learning. This can be done any number of ways, including reflective journals, response papers, or portfolios, either digital or paper. Students should write in their journals immediately after the conclusion of the IVC event, or within a day or so, to recap the major topics discussed and the lesson or lessons that may be connected. This activity helps the teacher develop an understanding of what students gained from the interaction as well as what connections students are making to lessons previously learned. A short, five-minute response paper or free-writing exercise helps you evaluate whether the student is learning anything new from the IVC or is able to apply prior knowledge to the event. Portfolios are living documents that provide a chronicle of the IVC events that have taken place throughout the school year, and they demonstrate a student's knowledge-based growth and skills development. Portfolios can also assist the teacher in assessing student interest in IVC events, guiding the teacher's preparation as the school year moves forward.

Finally, for program evaluation purposes, you may choose to document the time you spend in preparation for an IVC. In your lesson plan book, indicate date and time for each IVC and dedicate a column to track time spent during the preplanning and coordination processes. This reflective evaluation helps you better understand the process. As you review your lessons over time, you should see incremental improvement in time management and instructional design.

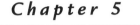

Chapter 5

Content
Design and Delivery

In previous chapters, we reviewed technical issues and planning activities that teachers interested in using IVC technology in the classroom must take into consideration. In this chapter, we'll talk about the most critical element of all: how to effectively design and deliver an IVC experience that will engage your students and support your overall curricular goals. Learning how to create and implement a successful IVC lesson will go a long way toward making you, as well as your school and district administration, feel comfortable adding this technology to your toolbox of standard teaching strategies and practices.

Pedagogy

The National Board for Professional Teaching Standards defines pedagogy as "the art or profession of teaching, or related to training or instruction" (AYA/ELA, 2004). Content pedagogy refers to the pedagogical (teaching) skills teachers use to impart the specialized knowledge or content of their subject area or areas. Effective teachers display a wide range of skills and abilities that lead to creating a learning environment where all students feel comfortable and are sure they can succeed both academically and personally. This complex combination of skills and abilities is integrated with the professional teaching standards that also include the essential knowledge, dispositions, and commitments that enable educators to practice at a high level.

Effective pedagogy for the integration of videoconferencing technology comprises several elements: the ability to use the equipment as a teaching tool, to design instructional materials that promote interactivity, and to manage students and activities from a distance. Videoconferencing is a teaching tool, not an end in itself. Like other technology-based instructional modalities, IVC can be, and should be, integrated into a teacher's repertoire to help the teacher transmit specific concepts and skills to students. Knowing how to use the equipment effectively and where to access IVC content is important, but the ways in which teachers infuse the technology into classroom instruction are the keys to successful implementation.

It isn't enough to attend a workshop in which you learn how to turn the IVC unit on, zoom in and out, and use the document camera. You must also learn how to develop a lesson plan that incorporates the videoconference itself. You need time to identify appropriate IVC content and determine where it will fit into your curricular plans. As McKenzie (2003) notes below, technology training, in and of itself, is not sufficient:

> Too often technology training has shown teachers how to use spreadsheets or PowerPoint while failing to demonstrate how these tools might impact learning in their fifth-grade classroom, their biology classroom, or their art classroom. Schools have offered few courses that focus on classroom management issues or ways to customize learning to match the interest, skills and needs of the learners. We have seen too little focus on curriculum rich strategies.

How can IVC technology help you impart knowledge and skills and engage your students in learning from a distance? Let's take a look at the following areas of pedagogy (as suggested by McKenzie):

- Student needs
- Classroom culture
- Instructional strategies
- Problem solving
- Professional development

Student Needs

A student's ability to negotiate virtual environments while building social infrastructures both online and in person is more essential today than ever. In addition to the social aspect of learning, students should become comfortable doing research beyond the textbook and building collaboration skills. The revision of ISTE's National Educational Technology Standards for Students (NETS•S) outlines these expectations. The more exposure students have to global peers within a classroom, the more prepared they are to enter college and the workforce.

Many students are exceptionally familiar with technology and are ready to see it used in more innovative ways in the classroom. Teachers who integrate IVC or blended (hybrid) lessons keep students more engaged and expose them to more than traditional instructional materials.

Comfortable with technology, students enjoy interacting with their peers via the Internet. Here, South Dakota fifth-graders interact with first-graders.

Teaching students how to use the technology they use on a regular basis helps them understand the usefulness of the technology. Students today use video cameras to post to online social networks, but when this use is introduced in the classroom, students may recognize a more beneficial application of the technology. In the contemporary classroom, the use of a communication technology such as IVC makes perfect sense. It's not a quantum leap for young people, it's just more of the same— and they like it. If IVC is used effectively, students will really connect with the content and want to do it again and again!

100% ENJOYMENT

In recent evaluations of more than 2,000 K–12 students who participated in an IVC program with the Virtual School at Vanderbilt University, 100% indicated they would like to do another videoconference.

Classroom Culture

It's important, of course, that teachers create a safe and supportive environment within the walls of their schoolroom. Students' emotional and social needs should be taken into consideration in the overall ebb and flow of the classroom community. These efforts become even more essential when a physical separation exists between teachers and students. In the daily IVC classroom, close communication between students, classroom facilitators, and the virtual teacher (teacher of record) is critical. Without a strong relationship, both students and teachers will become frustrated and may even believe the experience is a failure.

A 9/11 COLLABORATION

Linda Snapp, Distance Learning Coordinator; Allen ISD; Allen, Texas

Teachers and high school students in New Jersey and Texas collaborated via IVC to remember the events of September 11, 2001. An insightful dialogue was sparked in their first videoconference. Students talked about how the event affected their homes and communities and talked about President George W. Bush's war against terrorism.

In March 2003, following a successful fundraising campaign to finance the trip, 16 students and 5 adults from Allen, Texas, traveled to Linden, New Jersey, to visit their cohorts. Following on the heels of the earlier videoconferences and the exchange of e-mail addresses, this trip was a culminating activity for students who had forged meaningful relationships via the videoconferencing. A welcoming committee of school, city, fire, and police department officials met the Texas students, who then shadowed their counterparts around school. The following day they all boarded a bus to New York City.

The most touching experience was when the bus pulled up to Liberty and West streets. You could have heard a pin drop; the sight of the void that went down six levels took their breath away. The barricades were removed and our bus proceeded down a ramp, where we were met by New York City Port Authority officials. We were given the VIP treatment and taken into an observation room. There, the tragic story was recounted. We were then led to the platform that overlooked the clean-up process. This spot served as a memorial area, and our kids—from opposite sides of the country, of different faiths and ethnic groups— shed tears together and held each other. It was unforgettable.

It's of course difficult to keep your finger on the pulse of students when they're hundreds of miles away. Employing a virtual classroom coordinator will help keep communication channels open and will assist the teacher of record in creating a virtual classroom culture in which participants feel as if they belong. One strategy for maintaining the classroom community, especially during noninstructional time, is to establish an online chat time for small groups of students, or even between individual students, and to also encourage regular e-mail communication among all the members of the virtual classroom.

If you're using IVC for supplemental events, you'll discover these experiences can increase students' social skills with people outside their own communities or local cultures. It's one of the great benefits of producing and participating in multipoint videoconferences. The resulting opportunity for groups of students to see, hear, and interact with students and teachers from remote areas and ways of life becomes part of the learning experience.

HELLO FROM MICHIGAN

Kathy Jenkins, Distance Learning Coordinator
Newaygo County Regional Education Service Center; Fremont, Michigan

We've had videoconferencing in our county for about 10 years now. Up until two years ago, the only equipment we had was kept in videoconferencing rooms (one at each high school). We used these rooms for shared classes between five different school districts and for an occasional videoconference with a provider, such as a zoo, or with another class for a special project.

Then we purchased a portable system, and videoconferencing has really taken off! The system can be taken to any classroom in the five districts and set up pretty quickly. We've found that taking the equipment to the classroom works better than taking the students to the equipment. We've participated in many videoconferences with zoos, NASA, museums, and so forth. We've also participated in projects such as Read Across America. In addition, we've had some classrooms partner up for projects, such as sharing a presentation about their community or some other area of study. We've also had students who were penpals finally get to meet face-to-face during a videoconference. We use our system at least weekly, and some days are downright crazy in terms of getting the equipment where it needs to be for a videoconference because we're so busy!

If you're new to videoconferencing and ever want to connect with us for a demo for teachers or just to chat for a few minutes, I'd be happy to help you out. I've set up connections for staff meetings to just talk with teachers about what we've done and some of the great experiences we've had. You can reach me at kjenkins@ncresa.org.

Instructional Strategies

Incorporating virtual learning technologies into the classroom requires strategic planning. When you're planning a supplemental IVC, carefully consider when the program will likely have the greatest impact on student learning. For example, should a connection with a specific content provider be scheduled at the beginning of a unit, to pique students' interest and motivation, or should it be scheduled in the middle of a unit, once students have gained background knowledge on the topic? If you're considering the midpoint of a unit, you could bring in a content expert via IVC to discuss the topic in depth. Another option is to have your students develop a project and presentation to be shared with another group of students from another school who may be studying the same content area.

Pedagogical strategies for delivering daily IVC classes include integrating a variety of opportunities for student interaction and hands-on activities. Students should receive clear directions about what is expected from the class, from activity to activity. Ideally, instructional *segments* should be broken up into 10-minute intervals, and talking-head teacher lectures should be kept to a minimum. Your clarity of purpose, confidence, and leadership will keep instruction flowing smoothly and students engaged and on task.

Problem Solving

As technology goes, there's always the possibility of errors or breakdowns. We encourage you to always have a back-up plan on hand of something you can do in the classroom with your students, sans technology. For example, have students break up into small groups to conduct on-site research on the topic at hand.

In the case of supplemental IVCs, when you research content providers, remember to find out if they have a cancellation policy. How far in advance will you need to let them know if a program has to be canceled or rescheduled? If the provider cancels or their program turns out to be extremely poor in quality, will you get a refund for fees charged? If your camera or network lines fail, what alternative activity might be available to avoid student (and teacher) disappointment? Keep these potential issues in mind as you prepare for an IVC event for your students.

If the event is high profile, with a large budget and cast of characters, incorporate Plan B in your written lesson plan and prepare for those options before the big day arrives! There's always the possibility, for example, that a technical problem with the audio will prevent sites from hearing one another. Preparing some ready-made signs ahead of time to either hold up or place on the document camera will help you communicate with the other site and possibly resolve the problem. We also suggest having blank paper and markers ready for these special messages.

Professional Development

Teachers are, by trade, lifelong learners. While teacher colleges do a good job of imparting content knowledge, educational psychology, and teaching methodology, we all know real learning starts the moment we stand in front of our first group of students. We know students learn best when we're their coach rather than the "sage on stage." Students become active learners when we empower them with tools to guide them to knowledge, rather than employing teacher-centered skill, drill, and test. We know today's technology fosters global learning communities rather than village-centered learning communities. We've found over and over again that learning how to use a software application well doesn't necessarily ensure its effective deployment in day-to-day classroom instruction. IVC technology offers you access to professional development opportunities that can dramatically reduce the learning curve all teachers must go through.

WHAT ONE EDUCATOR DISCOVERED DURING HIS FIRST VIDEOCONFERENCE WORKSHOP

Nikos Theodosakis, Director in the Classroom Videoconference Workshop
www.thedirectorintheclassroom.com

My first videoconference/online workshop was with the Forney School District in Texas. The goal was to help educators explore the use of filmmaking in the classroom. They would learn to use filmmaking as a tool to engage learning, enhance curriculum, and develop lifelong thinking skills. Since we would share a monitor instead of a room, the images, timing, and flow had to be designed to be as engaging and informative as possible. I believe what made the workshop a success was each participant's ability to explore concise, relevant material over an extended time, rather than in the compressed format of a two-day workshop.

The obstacle of geography having been removed by the employment of distance technologies, we redesigned the workshop as a six-week online/videoconference course, where participants had more time to absorb, research, and think about what it was they were learning. They had time to form questions that related to their own specific work. Within a week after this workshop, I received an e-mail from the coordinator to say that teachers had already begun filmmaking projects in their classrooms. Learning can happen anywhere learning wants to happen.

Nikos Theodosakis presents a workshop on Filmmaking in the Classroom to a group of educators in the Forney School District in Texas.

We encourage you to seek out professional development opportunities that cover both the how-to and the pedagogy of videoconferencing in the classroom. Learning from other teachers who have had experience in using this modality in their own classrooms, who can share their tips and methods for success, is one effective avenue to access training at little or no expense. Talk to peers who have experience, or read accounts written by other teachers and virtual learning specialists. You can learn from their successes and mistakes. In our opinion, a great online support for educators with IVC-related questions is the Videoconferencing Collaboration Collage e-mail list sponsored by Knowledge Network Collaboration.

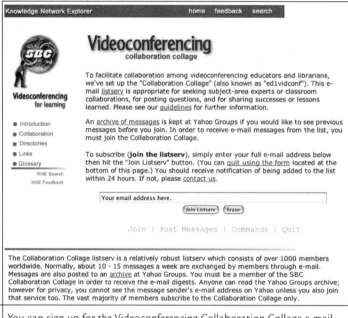

You can sign up for the Videoconferencing Collaboration Collage e-mail list at www.kn.att.com/wired/vidconf/ed1vidconf.html

Another source for professional development, whether it concerns matters such as distance learning, pedagogy, or future education trends, is the Center for Interactive Learning and Collaboration's Professional Development Center (www.cilc.org/c/consulting/professional_development.aspx). Your school can participate in many of their offerings over IVC or web-based collaborative technologies.

Instructional Design

Instructional design for virtual learning programs requires careful consideration of how students will benefit fully from the experience. How can your teaching objectives best be met through the application of IVC technology? When designing a lesson or syllabus for videoconferencing, the following elements should be fully spelled out:

- Lesson objectives
- Objectives for videoconference interaction
- Introductions

- Presentation of information
- Activities
- Assessment

Lesson Objectives

Whether you employ this technology as a daily teaching tool, an enhancement/enrichment experience, or a classroom-to-classroom collaborative tool, the objectives of any videoconference should mesh with your overall curriculum objectives. The IVC should not be separate from classroom instruction but, rather, an embedded component of the overall lesson.

For example, if you're studying the general history and impact of sports on American culture, a videoconference with, say, a basketball player might be a perfect addition to the lesson. As students learn about the early history and development of basketball in American culture, they're likely to experience a disconnect between the historical perspective and the perspective they've developed based on what they currently see on television. A videoconference with a college or professional basketball player who shares his experiences with the class can help students connect these two perspectives, giving them a chance to learn how the player practices and prepares for games, the sacrifices and training he or she must undergo, the advantages and disadvantages of fame, the difficulty of performing under a public spotlight, and so forth. The IVC provides a focus that integrates the technology into the existing curriculum; the face-to-face interaction of the videoconference can strengthen and deepen students' understanding of sports culture in America.

Don't forget that you can use additional online tools to prepare for the IVC or as an extension after the videoconference has occurred. When using these additional online tools, students have the flexibility to explore the content related to the IVC before and after the conference. Make sure that your online content is clearly related to the IVC topic and easily navigated.

Objectives for Videoconference Interaction

As noted previously in the example of videoconferencing with a basketball player, human interaction made possible by IVC can add tremendous depth and color to what otherwise might be a strictly academic lesson. Teachers should consider carefully how best to stimulate and manage this interaction to benefit students, and how to place both students and experts on a path that will lead to anticipated learning outcomes. One way to encourage this is to provide the expert with a list of key concepts, or talking points, before the videoconference. In the case of the lesson on the impact of sports on American culture, the teacher might want to direct the basketball player to focus his talk on specific issues most closely related to topics students have studied in class so that the videoconference doesn't become a recitation of game statistics or the basketball team's chances in the upcoming playoffs. Preparing the expert ahead of time will yield a much greater return on the overall value of the lesson.

In addition to preparing remote-site participants, you should work to manage interaction so that it's clear and concise. Certain rules must apply to the interaction. For example, students can't all speak at once or no one will be heard. Instead, facilitators at each site should state where it's located and who's making the comment before sharing questions, comments, or information. Sweeping gestures and fast movements should be avoided to reduce disruption in the video relay. Students should feel comfortable enough to speak freely, but they should also remain on task and share talk time. During the videoconference, the teacher's role is akin to that of an orchestra conductor: directing the action, focusing attention, modulating the tone and tempo, and inspiring all participants to perform to the best of their abilities.

Students may be directed to post to a blog or instant messaging site to record their questions and possibly have them answered online during the IVC. Using these tools in support of the IVC adds another dimension to the IVC experience.

FROM THE MANHATTAN THEATRE CLUB

Scott Merrick, LS Tech Coordinator/Teacher-in-residence
University School of Nashville; Nashville, Tennessee

One of the most noteworthy IVCs I've helped facilitate is University School of Nashville's long-running collaboration with the Theatrelink project, originating out of the Manhattan Theatre Club (MTC) in New York. As of this writing, drama teacher Gus Gillette and students are in our school's 4th year of work with Theatrelink.

High school classes all over the country work with the MTC artistic staff in New York to conceive and script a play, then each school passes their play off to another participating school, whose students produce and perform it. USN's students helped pioneer the delivery of the performances of the plays to their authors via IVC, as well as working with the MTC staff via IVC during the playwriting and production processes.

I maintain an IVC-related blog to archive our school's work in IVC (http://ivcatusn.blogspot.com), where you may find a post from 2006–07's collaboration (http://ivcatusn.blogspot.com/2006/05/theatrelink-2005-6-concludes.html).

Theatrelink's website is www.theatrelink.org/public/index.cfm.

USN is at http://usn.org, and I'm at http://scottmerrick.net.

Introductions

It's critical to set the stage before jumping into the content of the videoconference. This will help put the participants at ease and aid in communication. You can accomplish this by allowing time for introductions, and for even an icebreaker or two if this is the first time end users or students have participated in a videoconference. By giving people an opportunity to introduce themselves, you not only begin to develop a sense of virtual community, but you also demystify the technology through touch and utilization.

An example of a simple icebreaker that works well with IVC is to ask participants to take out of their purse, wallet, backpack, or notebook an item that represents something important about their lives or about them as a person. Then have them use their on-site document camera to share their objects and describe briefly how it relates to them. In the end, you'll all know each other a little better, and everyone will have had a chance to practice using the document camera. An icebreaker for middle and high school students may be to develop (through guided discussion, of course) ground rules for the IVC.

Presentation of Information

Your presentation might take the form of a lecture, a demonstration, a discussion, a staging of materials, or an interactive activity such as a science experiment. The staging should engage students and hold their attention. The entire videoconference should last at least 30 minutes, but no longer than 45 minutes. Separate your presentation into 10-minute segments by incorporating multiple preset camera angles, scheduling activities or adding video clips to break up the lecture. You can switch to discussion mode, have students answer questions, or turn to a hands-on activity. Provide students with written directions and materials prior to the videoconference. The presentation strategies section later in this chapter will provide you with a sample lesson plan that demonstrates how you might integrate interactive presentation strategies with use of the IVC functions.

INTERACTIVITY

Interactivity is an essential component of the videoconference, for it's the interaction that separates a videoconference from a video. You, as the teacher, can establish the interactive quality of the IVC by guiding introductions between all participating far-sites and your own site. Embed this in your lesson plan. During the introductions, remind students of appropriate IVC etiquette.

The Oregon Museum of Science and Industry presents a teacher workshop via IVC.

Activities

Activities should directly relate to the overall objective of the videoconference presentation and should reinforce concepts already learned. In order for students and teacher(s) to work together virtually, they must have previously established a relationship through the introduction process and by display of **tent signs** identifying their site/location.

TECHNICAL ASPECTS

Part of the instructional design process includes incorporating technical aspects of the IVC lesson, accounting for time needed to set up the class, check the equipment, and make the connection with each site.

Following is a good example of a videoconference activity that supports overall learning objectives:

The presenters, located at Mount Rushmore (South Dakota), are teaching students about the design and construction of the Mount Rushmore monument. They pause at a certain point and instruct students to use any tool at their disposal to carve an image of their state into a native rock. After 10 to 15 minutes, students share the carvings with the presenters, who comment both on the tools they used and the types of rocks they carved. Students are then asked to compare the tools available in the 21st century with the tools actually used to shape and carve Mount Rushmore. Students then collaborate with each far-site by working in small groups.

For large IVC classes or groups, activities or assignments should be identical for each far-site. Design IVC activities that lend themselves to the medium and to distance delivery. IVC may not be suitable for all lesson types. For example, a chemistry class might benefit greatly from speaking with an expert on the chemistry of plastics or viewing a new method for synthesizing them. However, to conduct a lab where students at both sites are working with burners and beakers and are focused on what is in front of them rather than on what is happening at the other site would not very well utilize the interactivity IVC offers. Students are not likely to benefit much from the technology in this instance. Keep a keen eye on your objectives. Make sure IVC will enhance learning, not inhibit it.

If students must work alone during an assignment, check with that site every 5 to 10 minutes to verify the connection and see if they might need further direction or assistance. Sharing work from one site to another can be facilitated by use of the document camera or the electronic whiteboard, allowing each student at each site to see a clear example of each other's work.

Assessment

Strategies for assessment could include questioning techniques, checklists documenting participation of various students, or surveys to document students' appreciation of the videoconference. Assessment might also take the form of an assignment related to the IVC; for example, connecting students from two different states and having them share each state's history. The two classes could then be asked to compare these histories. This helps raise learning to a higher level. Videoconferencing assessment is an important way to determine this modality's value for student instruction and access to resources.

The value of the videoconference should be separately assessed by everyone involved: the teacher, the near-site students, and the students or content provider at the far-site. Brief surveys or checklists can be used to determine these values. After each IVC event, the facilitator should send a debriefing e-mail to all locations. The e-mail should ask at least three questions related to the overall lesson objectives and how well they were met. All participants should assess their own contribution and the contribution of others. This type of self-assessment will increase interactivity during the next event. Students are more likely to improve their interaction skills if they recognize that there is a need for improvement and that better interaction ultimately benefits them. Teachers will modify and improve their preparation and planning if they know where to focus their efforts. Experts and content providers will do the same. The greater the interaction during the videoconference, the more likely it is that participants will acknowledge that learning occurred. If minimal interaction consistently occurs because of the content covered or the manner in which the content is presented, teachers should consider discontinuing the event or replacing it with another.

Learning objectives are assessed for IVC lessons just as with any other lesson. Learning outcomes are measured through the traditional methods listed above or through alternative assessment strategies, some of which we discussed earlier. Technology-specific objectives—technical issues and interactivity—can be measured through formal evaluation of the IVC event, but these should be looked at separately from learning objectives. For example, the assessment of a reading comprehension lesson that uses Reader Rabbit software should measure the level of reading comprehension rather than the use of the software. The same applies with this technology.

> ## KEEP IT SMALL
>
> The greater the number of students involved in a videoconference, the less opportunity they have to interact with each other and the teacher or presenter, so take care to limit numbers appropriately.

Summative assessment tools best measure the long-term effect IVC has on learning outcomes overall. These tools may include reflective journals, rubrics, self-assessments, portfolios, essays, timelines, and test items on traditional tests, and they will work for any use of IVC. If one teacher is teaching to two different locations, then a web-based course management tool such as *WebCT* or Blackboard may be a valuable assessment resource.

Instructional Strategies

As you're developing unit plans, consider which lessons are best suited for videoconferences. What topics in your curriculum plan could be enhanced by the addition of a videoconference? What could students learn by using this interactive technology that they couldn't learn using another method or tool? If you know of a special videoconference that will be available only at a certain time, how can you arrange your curriculum plan to make the best use of this educational resource?

If you're designing a unit on storytelling, for example, consider introducing the concept by having students participate in a storytelling videoconference. Front-loading a thematic unit with this kind of interactive exercise provides students with prior knowledge they can draw on when the process of storytelling is taught in the classroom. If you've completed a history unit with a focus on your state, consider connecting with a class from another state and have your students share what they've learned. Perhaps you've just volunteered to teach an AP science course next term to students in remote locations around your state. Whether you'll be taking your students on a one-time IVC excursion or teaching a daily IVC class, the strategies that follow will help you make the experience positive and successful for both you and your students.

Establishing the Learning Environment

Objectives and procedures should be clearly established, and introductions made, at the beginning of each videoconference. If multiple sites are involved, the teacher should take care of this prior to the start of the IVC. An explanation of the purpose of the videoconference should precede the introduction of the presenter or the start of the class.

NATURAL INTERACTION

There will be times when your students are so captivated by the presenter or teacher, or by the technology itself, that they'll forget their shyness, and a natural interaction will begin to flow.

Share your learning objectives and expectations with the class, and remind students of IVC procedures, protocols, etiquette, and possible limitations (we'll discuss these in detail in just a moment). Students new to IVC can benefit greatly from viewing experienced students interacting during an actual videoconference event. You could show video clips of other IVC events or have your students take part as "view only" participants during their first multi-point IVC.

It's not unusual for students to be shy or unusually quiet during their first IVC experience. Following are some of the many simple ways to get them to relax and interact during the videoconference:

- Ask students to write down questions ahead of time.
- Model interactive behavior.
- Give students time to adjust; don't push them too hard.
- Ask students to introduce themselves before the program or class begins.
- Start the IVC with an icebreaker, giving everyone a chance to use the technology and contribute to the discussion

These activities are all part of setting the stage for the event or class.

Presentation Strategies

The instructional power of interactive videoconferencing rests both in its ability to allow people to interact and communicate face-to-face and its capacity to facilitate the sharing of multimedia presentations across the miles. Whether your computer is internal to the IVC unit or is connected through a ***scan converter,*** IVC enables you to show and narrate PowerPoint presentations, visit websites, view documents, and utilize computer applications. Other peripheral input devices, such as the document camera, electronic whiteboard, and VCR, allow you to display objects (e.g., a computer processor microchip) or graphics (book pages), use the monitor as a whiteboard to generate lists or track ideas, or show video clips or entire films.

Once you've decided what you'll present via videoconference, we suggest you prepare a script that leads you smoothly through a series of activities that engage participants. When you've completed your script and are comfortable with it, carefully prepare, specific to IVC requisites, all the graphics and media you'll use. Most important, be prepared. Practice. Tape yourself while you're practicing or while you're actually delivering. This kind of direct feedback can be brutal and hard to watch, but it will be worth it. Practice in front of the camera until you feel comfortable. You may feel uneasy at first, but experience and practice will help.

To give you an idea of the preparation necessary, Appendix B features sample lesson plans and videoconferencing scripts for elementary, middle school, and high school grade units. As an example, the middle school lesson plan and script were prepared for a videoconference unit on South Dakota monuments, incorporating the concepts of technology tools and types of rock formations. It includes objectives, activities, evaluation ideas, and resources. Following the lesson plan is the script for the videoconference itself.

Pre-Conference Preparation

You'll need to attend to technical and instructional details before you're ready to begin your IVC class or event. Become familiar with the technology and practice using it, or have someone on hand who can use it. We assume that at this point you or your technical staff have already conducted a test call with the participating far-sites. Following are some additional tips that will ensure a smooth IVC setup:

- Arrive early.
- Confirm at least 30 minutes prior to the IVC that the system is powered on and ready to go.
- Confirm who's placing the call and have their contact information available if it's a network hub.
- Load all applications and the computer presentation ahead of time.
- Bookmark any websites you'll be using during class time.
- Arrange and confirm camera and microphone placements.

- Confirm that you have technical support and far-site contact information at your fingertips in case of problems.

- Check volume.

Projecting across the Miles

You'll need to adapt your performance style to the requirements of teaching and learning from a distance. These presentational tips may help:

- When you speak, project your voice. Speak a little slower than you might in normal conversation. Make an extra effort to enunciate clearly.

- If you have students both at your home-site and at far-sites, try to maintain consistent and equal eye contact with both groups. Look right into the student camera's eye.

- Wear comfortable clothing you feel good about, and keep jewelry and accessories to a minimum. Plaid dresses and ties with checks are a no-no. Wear bright, solid colors or soft pastels. Shades of blue are ideal.

> **LEARNERS' NEEDS**
>
> The teacher should be cognizant of the learners' needs and the nature of their interest in the subject (Zohoori, 1997).

- As you present, be animated and use normal hand gestures, but move slowly if you have to move around. Rapid movements can cause the video picture to pixilate or freeze at the receiving sites. Be mindful of your facial gestures, as remote students are looking for communication cues in different ways than they would be if you were in the same room.

- Keep the camera angle close to your face if you're talking.

- Remember: you don't want to be a talking head. Pace your presentation in short, varied segments, and employ a variety of visual materials.

- Don't employ a document in the conversation or instruction unless everyone has access to a copy, either physically or via the document camera.

- You might keep on hand a large happy face or a scowling one to use with the document camera to drive an emotion home across the miles.

- Keep an eye on the monitor so that you can have a sense of what the far-site students are receiving from you at any given time.

Other Tips for Effective, Trouble-Free Presentations

As we mentioned earlier, if you take time to set the stage for your class or presentation, you enhance your ability to communicate effectively and increase the likelihood of a seamless videoconference. Many new users make the mistake of jumping right into the presentation without taking time to introduce participants, explain the technology, and ensure that everyone involved understands what's going on and what to expect throughout the class or event. If your audience is confused or uncertain, you'll lose their attention in the first 10 minutes. Below are some suggestions for engaging IVC participants and keeping them engaged throughout the videoconference:

- Allow time prior to the start of the presentation to check microphones and video for each site.

- Review use of the equipment and establish methods of communication as well as protocols for interaction.

- Allow time for introductions; know who your audience is.

- Capture your audience's attention right away; guide the learning process.

- Set the stage; identify the important components of your material both at the beginning of the videoconference and at the end.

- Let students know what your objectives are and what their role is.

- Stop and ask for questions or feedback often; engage students frequently.

- Allow extra time for students to respond.

- State the learner's name as you interact during question and discussion periods.

- Use procedural, discussion, and evaluative questioning strategies.

- Observe the dynamic of your group in order to control interaction.

- Assess and address problems, instructional or technical, that arise as you proceed.

- Encourage students to let you know if they're experiencing difficulty hearing you or seeing you at any time during the IVC. This should be one of the roles of the far-site facilitators

Incorporating Graphics and Multimedia

Employ a variety of visuals in your IVC presentation whenever possible. We've listed below a few guidelines to follow as you prepare and use these materials:

- Videotapes should follow U.S. television standard NTSC.

- Slides and photographs should be presented in a horizontal format; avoid glossy pictures.

- Keep your graphic presentations simple.

- For easy viewing, use a font size ranging from 24 to 44 points.

- Fonts should be sans serif and bold.

- Keep text to 10 lines per page, 30 letters per line.

- Use pastel background colors and keep these consistent.

- Have a pad of pastel construction paper on hand for use on the document camera.

- When using the document camera, print clearly with fast-drying, bold, black, Sharpie pens.

> **DOCUMENT CAMERA**
>
> You can use the document camera to display photos, slides, posters, book pages, maps, newspaper articles, models, specimens, and just about anything that doesn't leak or ooze.

You'll learn through experience, of course, what works best for you and what you should do differently the next time. You'll also discover quickly that videoconferencing has a way of magnifying every little slip or oversight. If you're not prepared, it's hard to wing it. A final word of caution: just because you're a great classroom teacher doesn't mean you can present an IVC class or event without careful preparation and practice.

Interaction Strategies

Interactive videoconferencing provides students, teachers, and other presenters with a live venue through which people separated by great distances can come together in real time. Successful IVC relies on active participation and the easy flow of conversation. Prepare for success by explaining to your students the importance of body language and tone of voice. Explain also how students at the far-sites will respond to these cues.

HANDS-ON ACTIVITIES

To enhance the interactive process, incorporate hands-on activities for students as part of the IVC presentation or as part of the pre-IVC or post-IVC measures. Student activities that take place after the IVC class or event should reinforce contextual information provided during the IVC.

To keep the exchange dynamic and interesting for students, you might have them complete a project or presentation prior to the IVC and share the results with the far-site participants during the videoconference. Students could create posters or other graphic materials to share via the document camera. One class we know of created an entire model city and shared their city design. An exchange can work the other way, too—as a response to the IVC experience. Students could write a reflective essay about a story they heard during a videoconference, for example, telling the presenter how they felt as they were listening to the story.

Eliciting student communication during a videoconference is a challenge that can be overcome by using effective interaction and feedback strategies. Consider incorporating some of these strategies:

- Call on individual students by name.
- Have students keep a journal during the class and share one entry before the close of IVC.
- Use the far-site facilitator to assist with student participation.
- Ask students to formulate a written comment or reflection (perhaps in small groups at each site) to share with the virtual group via the document camera.
- Utilize student leaders.
- Reinforce interaction with immediate follow-up or praise, or both.
- Personalize your presentation by relating information directly to those at the far-site; use the name of their school, or mention activities or events they may be involved in.
- Use humor, anecdotes, and natural break periods to help everyone relax.
- Periodically ask for feedback on the process.

- Be responsive; facilitate interactivity.

- Take your time; make sure your pacing is appropriate for the audience.

- Know when to move on to the next segment by keeping an eye on the students in your monitor. Are they talking to each other or falling asleep?

- Use supplemental communication tools such as e-mail, websites, e-mail lists, and chat rooms.

- Pace your presentation and allow time for off-camera activities, followed by report-back sessions for students.

Rowena Gerber's students at Miami Day School share snake stories with students at a remote site.

Classroom Management Protocols for IVC

As the teacher or presenter, you're responsible for establishing the tone and managerial protocols for your IVC class or event. At the beginning of the term or the start of an IVC event, outline the ground rules for all participants. You can reinforce this critical information by providing a checklist prior to the IVC. Successful and well-managed videoconferences have student protocols as well as teacher protocols. Following are a few to abide by:

- Arrange and complete introductions before the start of an IVC.

- Make sure site and name tent signs are visible and readable from a distance.

- Assume at all times that the camera and microphones are live.

- Adhere to microphone courtesy rules, such as keeping microphones turned to the off position unless speaking, as established by the teacher or presenter at the start of class.

- Identify yourself and your location before asking or answering a question.

- Acknowledge (as a teacher or presenter) that a question has been asked, and state by whom, before answering and confirming the answer.

- Show respect for the teacher or presenter by not chatting during the IVC; even when the microphone is muted, the teacher can still see you.

- Remain seated during the IVC unless instructed to get up and move around.

- Be attentive; do not eat food or work on other assignments during an IVC.

- Wait an extra 20 to 30 seconds for a response when interacting via IVC to allow for the time lag built into most IVC setups.

- Have with you, before the IVC begins, all materials you will need for the class.

The establishment of such protocols will prevent the IVC teacher of record from having to stop the presentation frequently to attend to procedural issues. It will also help avoid the natural frustration that presenters may feel if participants don't act as if they're engaged. Establishing the rules ahead of time helps students understand what's expected of them during the videoconference.

IVC Etiquette

Most of the protocol rules suggested in the previous section support commonsense rules of etiquette. But since failure to establish these guidelines can ruin an IVC, or your experience as an IVC teacher or presenter, a few additional guiding principles for videoconferencing etiquette follow:

- As the teacher or presenter, remember to regularly acknowledge all participating sites.

- Participants should be mindful not to tune out the TV.

- Participants should not always expect to be entertained; this is not a *Star Trek* episode.

- Participants should not hog the microphone.

- Everyone should be aware of, and respectful of, IVC protocol as established by the teacher or presenter.

- Thank-yous and good-byes should complete each interactive videoconference.

Though you're not in the same room with your virtual learning students, you're still responsible for establishing and maintaining authority in your virtual classroom. Your far-site facilitator plays a key role, however, in keeping students on task, making sure they have required materials on hand, and ensuring that activities are completed and assignments returned to you in a timely fashion.

ONLINE CLASSES SUPPORT NETWORKING AND COLLABORATION

Janine Lim, Instructional Technology Consultant
Berrien RESD; Berrien Springs, Michigan

Berrien RESD has offered online classes supporting videoconferencing since 2003. Participants from across the United States have attended these classes, and even from Argentina, Canada, Costa Rica, and the United Kingdom.

Planning Interactive Curriculum Connections is an introduction to videoconferencing and includes how to connect to content providers and prepare for a quality videoconference experience. Kid2Kid Videoconference Connections takes participants step by step through the process of planning and implementing a videoconference project. Participants always appreciate the networking with classmates. In the words of one participant, "It was a very interesting class that was easily adjusted to the different levels of knowledge of the students. I like how geographically diverse the students were. The ideas were creative and interesting." Another coordinator said, "I'm so glad this class was offered. I've been able to receive some really great information. The information I received was not only great for me, but a lot of the content can be passed on to other teachers. Hopefully, this will get more teachers involved in this wonderful technology."

Participants in the class have continued on to create regional and statewide projects for their own service areas.

www.remc11.k12.mi.us/dl/picc/

www.remc11.k12.mi.us/dl/k2k/

The existence of a far-site facilitator should not give you a false sense of security. It's up to you to develop a relationship with participants, familiarizing yourself with their needs and shortcomings and responding to these in an appropriate way. Regular phone or e-mail office hours can help maintain open lines of communication. If you're teaching a daily IVC class, you'll want to respond immediately and individually to students who may either be having problems or causing problems. For a daily class, we also suggest that if at all possible you conduct at least one on-site visit to each far-site classroom during the course of the term or semester. An in-person meeting will help you establish a relationship with each student and ultimately make the job of virtual classroom management easier.

Post-IVC Evaluation

Evaluation of the interactive videoconference should occur on two levels: first, attempt to evaluate student learning; secondly, evaluate the use of the IVC technology. For supplemental content providers especially, the post-IVC evaluation will be an important indicator of the program's success and effectiveness. If you're a receiving site, be sure to complete any requested feedback and evaluation forms and return them promptly to the provider. Sample evaluation forms are provided in Appendix A.

The technology itself should be evaluated using a checklist or a comments sheet to indicate any problems that occurred during the videoconference setup, connection, or shutdown. Indicate the response time on the feedback form if tech support was called upon. This information will help you and the tech department during subsequent planning procedures.

Although content, rather than technology, should always be the driving force, the reality is: when the technology fails, the lesson suffers. Therefore, with all of the variables involved in conducting an IVC in the classroom, we recommend conducting test calls and preparing all participants with back-up plans. Clear communication of dates, times, and expectations can often minimize any technical difficulties that may arise, giving participants the time they need to work through the details of the connection.

Copyright Information for Interactive Videoconferencing

If you're designing or incorporating media content into your IVC, be informed about and consider copyright restrictions:

- As you prepare multimedia presentations, keep in mind that content material from other sources can be (and likely is) copyright protected.
- Original multimedia works are copyright protected.
- Commercial use of copyrighted material must have copyright permission.
- Copyright laws must become familiar to you (see below).
- Copyright guidelines set up by your school must be followed.

The Digital Millennium Copyright Act of 1998 (1998) was passed to revise copyright and intellectual property laws to meet the new legal challenges posed by digital media, computer networks, and the Internet. Because of restrictions imposed on education through this act, the Technology, Education and Copyright Harmonization (TEACH) Act of 2001 (2002) was subsequently passed.

The TEACH Act provides educators with alternatives to the Digital Millennium Copyright Act when using copyrighted materials for the purpose of instruction. Terms and conditions within the Digital Millennium Copyright Act were redefined by the TEACH Act.

Therefore, the TEACH Act is the predominant legislation dictating the use of copyrighted materials for educational purposes. The TEACH Act specifically addresses instructional activities distributed via digital networks but does not exempt teachers from all of the scrupulous requirements of the Digital Millennium Copyright Act; no longer can teachers use copyrighted materials without following the procedures outlined in the TEACH Act.

It should be noted that teachers are not sheltered from legal consequences by claiming they were not aware of the law or that it was an accident. Under the TEACH Act, educational institutions must provide guidelines for the use of copyrighted material.

Copyright protection has expanded with advancements in digital networks. Copyright protection acknowledges that the "original work of authorship" of such works as writings, images, artworks, videotapes, musical works, sound recordings, motion pictures, computer programs and other works are protected by copyright law (Crews, 2003, p. 8). Works that are in the public domain are not registered for copyright and therefore are readily accessible for instructional distribution. The copyright of any piece of work is in effect during the life of the author plus 70 years. Plainly put, few works are not protected by copyright.

Educators have long felt secure about the use of copyrighted materials under the umbrella of "fair use," but this is limited to face-to-face teaching in a traditional classroom environment (Crews, 2003). This sense of security is somewhat false with the passing of the newest copyright laws. For the purpose of videoconferencing technology, copyright laws related to distance education are most relevant. The rules of distance education are most strict when it comes to fair use, as materials uploaded to websites or transmitted through digital networks can be accessed by people other than the intended instructional audience.

Discretion should be taken when using copyrighted works during ***point-to-point videoconferencing*** or multipoint videoconferencing. This is especially important if the videoconference will be taped or streamed.

The TEACH act supports permission of copyrighted works in the context of "mediated instructional activities" but prohibits conversion of analog materials into digital formats (Crews, 2003, pp. 4, 10). The TEACH Act requires instructors to plan and conduct the distance activity as transmitted—even more reason to include the videoconference in the context of a lesson. "Mediated instructional" activities assumes the copyrighted works are integral to the teaching of the lesson.

Before creating a digital copy of the videoconference or before streaming the live videoconference, the following steps are recommended:

- Limit the amount of copyrighted materials used in the videoconference.
- Reference all copyrighted materials used under the auspices of fair use.
- When in doubt, contact the person or agency owning the copyright and ask permission to use the material for a videoconference that will be taped or streamed.
- Copyrighted materials should be used solely for the purpose of instruction and under the supervision of an instructor.
- If a person other than the instructor is offering a lesson to your class via IVC, review any copyrighted materials intended for the videoconference and ask to see permissions.

Copyright laws regulating a traditional face-to-face classroom would be applicable during a live videoconference provided the videoconference is not being taped or streamed. It's only when the videoconference becomes a digital media that the statute prohibits unauthorized broadcasting of protected works. Nevertheless, it's best to credit any copyrighted works used during a videoconference for the purpose of instruction. It's recommended that works not relevant to instruction should be forfeited.

A Fair Use Checklist is provided in Appendix A. To access more information on copyright related to distance education, please visit the websites of either the American Library Association (www.ala.org) or the U.S. Copyright Office (www.copyright.gov).

Chapter 6

The Future of Videoconferencing

Since the publication of the first edition of *Videoconferencing for K–12 Classrooms* in 2004, the use of virtual communication tools in K–12 and higher education classrooms has evolved to accommodate a mix of virtual instructional tools.

Educators are discovering that interactive videoconferencing as an instructional tool can be enhanced by the use of collaborative online software and web-based courses. These modalities are not new, especially for higher education, but use of collaborative software and web-based courses is gaining momentum in many K–12 classrooms and school districts throughout the country. web 2.0, virtual learning communities, virtual schools, and online learning are a few samples of how technology is changing the face of the classroom.

Planning collaborative activities effectively "builds supportive classroom communities, which, in turn, increases self-esteem and academic performance" (Willis, 2007, p. 5). Because we live in a knowledge-based economy, students need more opportunities to engage in learning experiences with other learners on a global scale in order to be successful in their future workplace. Collaborative projects that envelop online tools, videoconferencing, and print-rich materials assure students are well prepared (McAnear, 2007). Teachers who embrace tools geared toward preparing students for the responsibility of "digital citizenship" help prepare them for a world beyond the Internet we know today.

Blended Learning

Blended learning is a term that describes learning that mixes various event-based activities, including face-to-face classrooms, live e-learning, and self-paced learning (Bershin, 2004). Blended learning has emerged as a catch phrase that also refers to the deployment of a variety of communications software representing a number of teaching and learning solutions. IVC practitioners now have resources and tools readily available to blend face-to-face (synchronous) instruction with a menu of *asynchronous communication* tools. The result has been the development of virtual learning communities and instructional platforms, both in the classroom and beyond district boundaries.

Challenges of Blended Learning

- Success is dependent on regular and predictable communication of participants.
- Facilitators must understand strategies to engage and involve participants.
- Guidelines must be clear.
- There is risk of using technology for technology's sake.
- The learning curve may be time-consuming for classroom teachers.
- There is need for technology support.

Advantages of Blended Learning

- It encourages collaborative thinking and decision making.
- Students learn cooperation.
- It provides a forum for participants.
- Participants develop a sense of belonging and responsibility to others.
- It offers access to far-reaching resources.
- Community can be drawn together from almost anywhere, serving a variety of instructional purposes.
- Instruction is student centered rather than teacher centered.
- It fosters collaboration rather than isolation.
- Students acquire global awareness.

Internet2

Imagine a videoconference with digital video quality and no audio delay, courtesy of an Internet connection at 100 *gigabits* per second—400 times faster than most broadband connections available to home users today. As futuristic as this scenario sounds, it's actually already a reality—the reality of Internet2. Internet2 is a consortium of 248 universities working in partnership with industry and government to develop and deploy advanced network applications and technologies, accelerating the creation of tomorrow's Internet.

The Internet we all know and use today is the first generation Internet, shared with millions of commercial users across the country. When the Internet was born in the 1970s, it was used primarily by universities and government agencies to send data over long distances. Network traffic increased slowly until the advent of the World Wide Web and the first web browsers in the early 1990s, when personal and commercial usage increased exponentially across the country and around the world. As commercial usage of the Internet snowballed, the original network no longer adequately served the needs of universities, which still had to deliver huge packets of data to other universities. This led to the development of Internet2.

> ### INTERNET2 FOR K-12
>
> In partnership with Ciena, Infinera, Level 3 Communications, Juniper Networks, and the Internet2 NOC at Indiana University, Internet2 has completed the final transition steps in the rollout of the new Internet2 Network, which boasts speeds up to 100 gigabits per second and IP v.6 capablility.

Internet2 is the result of a partnership among academic institutions, high tech industries, and government agencies, just as the original Internet was. The primary goals of Internet2are to:

- Create a leading-edge network capable of serving the needs of the national research community

- Enable revolutionary Internet applications

- Ensure the rapid transfer of new network services and applications to the broader Internet community

Today, Internet2 is open to public and private colleges and universities, K–12 school districts, technical and trade schools, state and regional educational organizations, museums, art galleries, and hospitals. Examples include statewide K–12 networks, community college networks, and similar educational organization collectives. As of April 2007, more than 38 state education networks had applied for and received Sponsored Education Group Participant (SEGP) status from Internet2. As of the writing of this book, in these 38 states about 9,800 K–20 institutions are online via Internet2, as well as 35,890 K–12 schools; 3,325 public libraries; 1,683 community colleges and universities; and 48 museums, zoos, aquariums, and science centers.

Internet2 access must be sponsored by a higher education Internet2 member in the K–12 schools' and education partners' state. Furthermore, for a state aggregate to successfully apply for SEGP status, the following is recommended:

- Ideally, all Internet2 regular members in the state should be involved in discussions preliminary to an application; Internet2 encourages statewide collaboration among Internet2 members.

- Applicants should be able to document present and future education projects that would benefit from the Internet2 connection.

- A state network should exist (or be emerging) that can connect to the current Internet2 backbone and meet the Abilene Network's Conditions of Use (CoU).

- The sponsor(s) for the SEGP should ideally submit the application to Internet2 on behalf of the statewide education network.

- Finally, the connector for the SEGP is responsible for an annual SEGP fee to Internet2, which is $30,000 + $2,000 × the number of delegates the state sends to the U.S. House of Representatives.

A number of good reasons for a state to seek SEGP status and connect its schools to Internet2 include the following:

- Access to the most advanced, high-performance network in the world

- Participation in the development of advanced applications targeted for the K–12 community (according to the Internet2 website, Internet2 is the "killer app" for interactive videoconferencing)

- Improved IVC quality using ISDN or IP-1 connections, ensuring a seamless IVC

- Mobility of videoconference units (the IVC unit will be able to connect to any Internet jack in a school building)

- Increased K–12 access to university resources

- ***Real-time access*** to such remote instruments as university telescopes and electron microscopes

- Ability to interact in real time with remotely located groups

Oakland University and Port Huron Northern High School
share jazz over Internet2.

ALL THAT JAZZ

Michael Maison, Media/Technology Coordinator
St. Clair County Intermediate School District; Port Huron, Michigan

Oakland University (Rochester, Michigan) and St. Clair Intermediate School District joined forces to host a musical event combining collegiate and high school jazz musicians. Students and band conductor Catherine Trudeau from Port Huron Northern High School volunteered to participate. Professor Danny Jordon took the lead at Oakland University.

St. Clair ISD's role was to bring these two groups together and engineer the technology that would be used for the event. Internet2 and MPEG2 codecs brought this jazz activity to life on October 18, 2002. The professor coordinated the session in cooperation with the high school band conductor. The musicians presented a three-segment session—an improvisational piece, a period of formal instruction from the professor as both groups played jazz scales, and a fully orchestrated piece selected by the high school students.

Both groups of musicians played from their local facilities, miles apart. A live audience at the university watched the event. The common denominator was Internet2, and all participants experienced new possibilities using today's technology.

As we've mentioned, hundreds of museums, art and science centers, and historical sites have begun to offer educational content to schools via IVC. These institutions, as well as K–12 schools, are eligible for Internet2 membership. A school that has an Internet2 connection can link up to a museum with Internet2 connectivity via a high-quality audio/video feed, with practically no cost for the connection. Currently, this is possible in only some schools and with some content providers. The day may soon come when this connectivity is universal for educational organizations.

One interesting Internet2 project is the Globalization Initiative originating from the University of Missouri (Columbia) and the Missouri Research and Education Network (MOREnet). This venture has created a global learning community using advanced technologies and Internet2 to develop and foster school and community relationships, promote cross-cultural learning, and facilitate comprehensive school improvement programs. To date, four schools in Taipei, Taiwan, are connected with K–12 schools in Missouri as well as with University of Missouri faculty and preservice teachers.

INTERNET3

Universities have already begun work on Internet3!

Streaming Compressed Video

In the past we've been able to download videos such as news clips or even watch them as they're streamed to our Internet-connected computer. These downloads and streams have often been choppy and unsatisfactory in their audio or video quality. With higher bandwidth capabilities, improvement of streaming technology, and advanced software applications for desktop computers, video streams are becoming more accessible. Teachers, students, and parents in New York, for example, can access 20,000 video clips to download or stream on the Internet. Videos are searchable by keyword, subject area, grade level, or New York State Learning Standard. Texas, Georgia, Florida, Alabama, Tennessee, North Carolina, South Carolina, Oregon, and South Dakota are just a few of the states that maintain similar databases for videoconference content. No cost is involved in accessing many of these resources; however, if you decide to contact a content provider listed in the database, the IVC event may involve a fee. A comprehensive list of content provider sites, including statewide resources, is included in Chapter 7.

STREAMING

Some content providers are now adding streaming capability to their websites and interactive videoconference offerings. Once a video has been streamed, it can then be archived for future viewing.

The limitation of streaming video as opposed to true interactive videoconferencing is that participants cannot see or hear the students in the videoconference, eliminating the face-to-face interaction. Some companies have developed creative mechanisms that allow limited interactivity during a live stream. For example, the Fairfax Network, in Fairfax County, Virginia, hosts several streaming video programs, including one called Meet the Author. Students in Grades 7–12 sign up to hear Walter Dean Myers discuss the writing process and explain character development. During the live streamed program, students call in with questions for the author.

Teachers can benefit, too. For instance, one state's Department of Education provides live professional development, via interactive videoconference, to teachers and administrators throughout the state. For those unable to access a videoconference site, the IVC workshop is streamed to the Internet and can be accessed live via a desktop computer. An e-mail address allows streaming participants to send in questions to the presenter as the videoconference workshop is in session. For those unable to participate in either of the live modalities, an archived version of the IVC is posted on the department's website for anytime, anyplace viewing. Many of these kinds of e-learning programs are emerging, and professional development opportunities brought directly to a teacher's desktop computer via streaming video technology will soon be commonplace throughout the world.

Streaming video allows a school to purchase a live IVC event through a content provider and then stream it to all classrooms—without waiting for a download. Above is a videoconferenced presentation from the Milwaukee (Wisconsin) Public Museum.

Streaming video is superior to the downloadable videos of the past. You don't have to wait to watch the video while the file downloads to your computer; it loads, buffers, and begins to play in seconds. New developments in video streaming make this an efficient and cost-effective instructional tool. Streaming IVC allows a grade level to purchase an IVC event through a content provider and then stream the event to all sections of the grade level. This generally isn't a problem if you let the content provider know in advance what your intentions are. Remember, of course, that the person or institution that developed and delivered the material retains the copyright. If you capture this material without permission and redistribute it to a large group, you're most likely in violation of copyright.

It's easy to confuse an archived video stream with a downloadable video clip, but the two have differences. An archived stream usually represents material that was initially delivered in real time and captured to make it available through a secure server to anyone not able to participate in the live event. Video clips, on the other hand, are typically recorded and delivered asynchronously via the web. Regardless of the nature of the stream, however, if you're redistributing the material it's best to ask permission from the copyright holder.

Applications for Alternative Education

Deaf educators are some of the primary users of video-conferencing technology. In several states, these special educators use ***webcasting*** and video interpreting for curriculum development. Deaf students can use sign language via videoconferencing to communicate with other deaf students.

EMERGING APPLICATIONS

We are beginning to see the integration of synchronous and asynchronous applications. Live class presentations are now easily captured on "content servers," which can, in turn, be used to post archived video content on websites such as ITunes University, which is then downloadable to an IPod or other MP3 player. Look for future integration of video archives with learning management systems such as Blackboard and Moodle, too.

Virtual Learning Communities

Virtual learning communities broaden the learning environment to include people and resources beyond the boundaries of the classroom and the school district. Many students already participate in social networks. By posting images and text about their interests online, students connect with other students throughout the world. Many students never meet the friends they have online but they feel very connected to them because of the nature of the conversations they post or the video chats they participate in on an almost daily basis. Schools may shy away from supporting such tools but many technologists argue that it is better to teach students how to navigate these social networks than to leave them to learn on their own (Andrews, Smyth, Tynan, Vale, & Caladine, 2008).

Today, more and more teachers are participating in online professional development opportunities that include both web-based and videoconferencing modalities. Participation in distance professional development helps teachers become more familiar with both synchronous (IVC) and asynchronous (web-based) tools to support all kinds of programs and projects. The concept of online communities will continue to emerge over the coming decades and will be supported both by videoconferencing and web-based technologies, providing access and opportunities for all kinds of learning. The applications for K–12 students includes project-based learning activities and access to curriculum-based resources for both teachers and students.

In some states, juvenile detention lockup schools are using the technology to access content beyond the walls of the school. In another application, probation officers can meet with detained students via IVC and avoid incurring travel time to the school.

Additionally, rural schools can use videoconferencing for virtual counseling, virtual medical care, and other judicial and remote medical treatment purposes.

SOUTHERN OREGON'S "EXTENDING CAREER OPTIONS FOR K–12 STUDENTS" (ECORS) PROJECT

This pilot distance learning project, sponsored by the Southern Oregon Education Service District (SOESD) and funded by a United States Department of Agriculture (USDA) Rural Utilities Service (RUS) grant, launched in the summer of 2007.

SOESD's coordinator of technology and media services, Jay Matheson, procured an RUS grant to support the acquisition of mobile IVC Tandberg units for 17 schools in three counties located in a 14,000 square-mile region of Southern Oregon. The units will serve as many as 4,000 students and teachers in all grade levels. In addition to the Tandberg units, the grant supports content development and acquisition in support of the ECORS project.

During the first year of the three-year project, teachers are learning how to apply videoconferencing in the classroom to guide their students in accessing science, technology, engineering, and math (STEM) professionals from across the country. These rural students will connect with real-life professionals to expand their knowledge of career opportunities, requirements needed to prepare for certain career paths, and those who are already part of those worlds. They'll have access to people and places far beyond their remote rural communities.

Project teachers and leaders are taking part in a WebCT step-by-step training and participation guide, staffed daily by project leaders and facilitators. The result is a dynamic professional development virtual learning community. A blended learning toolbox, provided through the WebCT site, supports teachers' participation in the project. They use personal blogs to reflect upon and share their project activities. A community wiki allows participants to collaborate on the construction of a set of best practices. The WebCT discussion forum supports the community through ongoing conversations about what's working, sharing ideas and resources and getting to know each other as virtual community members. A virtual learning community home page serves as an online teachers lounge. The virtual community provides access to a wealth of project- and content-based resources.

In the process, these teachers are becoming experienced users of technologies that are already a critical component of the world of work into which their students will one day enter.

In years 2 and 3 of the project, participating classrooms connect with STEM professionals through IVC and web-based instructional tools. Professional partners serve as career mentors and role models. The WebCT project guide and virtual community provides participants with lists of resources and information about how to develop virtual partnerships in support of career awareness opportunities for their students.

Teachers benefit:

- From training and practice that help them integrate blended distance learning events and projects into existing curriculum. Each participant has access to a list of IVC content providers via the Center for Interactive Learning Collaboration (CILC).

- From opportunities to connect, on a daily basis and from their own classrooms, with project partners and leaders. The WebCT site is staffed daily by project facilitators.

Students benefit:

- From access to real professionals who would otherwise be outside their reach. Local and national IVC content partnerships are provided to all participating teachers. Teachers are asked to use the technology to earn "eBucks" to purchase the IVC content, including virtual field trips, virtual workshops, and even virtual professional development content.

- From exposure to a variety of career path experiences.

- From meeting and interacting with role models beyond their rural communities.

- From the opportunity to apply emerging technologies they will need proficiency in for college and the workplace.

Project participants met face-to-face for a two-day workshop during the week before the start of school. Teachers who attended were selected from participating schools to train as school-based project leaders in a "train-the-trainer" professional development model. The workshop provided the connections and vision necessary for the kickoff of this unique virtual learning project.

Virginia Petitt, online specialist for SOESD, had this to say about ECORS:

> ECORS is an innovative project designed to deliver career path education via distance learning to 17 small rural schools in Southern Oregon. A blended program incorporating both online and videoconferencing technologies, ECORS was designed by Southern Oregon Education Service District and funded by a grant from the USDA Rural Development Distance Learning Grant Program and local matching funds. The goal of the ECORS project is to expand students' career potential by exposing them to a broad range of real world career paths that may not exist in their rural area. Professional development in the use of videoconferencing, online learning, and technology integration is delivered to teachers via videoconferencing and online to help them use the cutting-edge tools provided by the grant. Teachers have also formed a professional learning community to connect across distances to share ideas, resources, and strategies in implementing this project, which helps students meet Oregon's new state requirements for graduation.

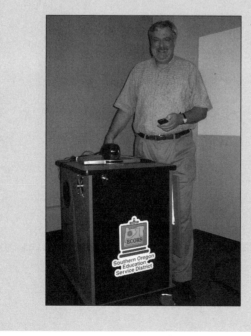

Jay Matheson shows off the customized mobile Tandberg IVC cart he designed for use in the ECORS project.

Virtual Learning Environments

An article on emerging technologies states that "distance education should invent its future by rethinking fundamental assumptions about teaching and learning" (Dede, 1996, p. 2). As technology has become more accessible in our classrooms, we're modifying and adapting our pedagogy. In the future, there should be no distinction between distance and traditional classrooms; all learning environments should be equal. Through this lens, the fundamental assumptions of what education is to our society will become a much broader process, one that embraces knowledge.

Virtual learning environments are steadily becoming more widely accepted. Virtual high schools and myriad online degree programs are slowly but surely becoming part of mainstream education. To date, close to half the states in the nation have in place state-sanctioned virtual schools. Many states, if not all, are still grappling with the need to establish virtual learning policies, standards, and teacher training. Instructional staff and technology staff are struggling to come together in this planning process. To facilitate new ways of accessing and delivering instruction, many states are designing and implementing a web-based portal or access point where information about all of the state's virtual learning programs is available to interested learners.

Virtual learning environments are more accepted today in part because technologies have emerged to meet the demands of the virtual classroom, improving access and interaction. The growth and stabilization of high-quality video networks is creating an infrastructure conducive to virtual education opportunities for all learners.

In a virtual learning environment, students log in and access their course through a dedicated website. Course content, quizzes, assignments, presentations, discussion, and chat are examples of application features associated with online course delivery. Students have access anytime and anywhere so that they can select the appropriate learning environment and time frame for their individual learning styles and personal schedules. Many virtual course development tools are already available: applications such as HorizonLive, Respondus, CamStudio, and Impatica are examples of programs available to virtual teachers who are creating online courses. Learning Management Systems (LMS) such as WebCT and Blackboard are low-cost options for virtual education program delivery and implementation.

Virtual course delivery offers K–12 students an alternative route to a high school degree. It also offers teachers and districts a new way to access professional development programs. Some colleges of education have modified their education methods courses for virtual delivery, and student teaching is now often monitored and observed using IVC technologies.

VIRTUAL NECC

The 2007 National Educational Computing Conference was a significant year for ISTE. This is the year that NECC went virtual! The NECC Virtual Learning Community for educators was coordinated by members of the NECC program committee and allowed teachers in South Georgia to participate in NECC workshops and sessions without driving to Atlanta. Participants used online chat tools and videoconferencing to enjoy a slice of the NECC experience. ISTE members were also invited to participate in Second Life, a multiuser virtual environment.

LOWER KUSKOKWIM SCHOOL DISTRICT: SHARED CLASSES

Pam Lloyd, Senior Program Manager; GCI SchoolAccess; Anchorage, Alaska

The Lower Kuskokwim School District (LKSD) is one of Alaska's largest rural school districts, servicing an area roughly the size of West Virginia. The district's 352 teachers and numerous paraprofessionals serve approximately 3,800 students in kindergarten through Grade 12. Because of the district's size and rural location, staffing every school with specialists in every field is a challenge.

LKSD has partnered with GCI SchoolAccess to provide videoconferencing capabilities to classrooms around the district. By availing themselves of the opportunities presented through videoconferencing, teachers in LKSD can be 21st-century educators, regardless of their location. Through GCI SchoolAccess, educators can open doors to new content and have the opportunity to develop students' 21st-century skills: communication, critical thinking, technology literacy, problem solving, creativity, and self-direction. Together, the Lower Kuskokwim School District and GCI SchoolAccess are leading the way in integrating technology into the classroom and providing students and educators with incredible learning opportunities.

Online Learning

Online learning refers to the distance learning format that uses the Internet to deliver instruction and provide opportunities for interaction among students (Davis & Niederhauser, 2007). Teachers may use course management software such as Blackboard or Moodle to develop courses or extension lessons. These courses are often developed by instructional designers and taught by several different teachers. Extension lessons may be developed by instructional designers and made available to classroom teachers through textbook supplemental resource materials or subscription to online education sites.

Virtual classroom refers to the learning context that is established in online learning environments, while virtual schooling includes all of the elements associated with learning in an online environment (Davis & Niederhauser, 2007). Any given school may offer a virtual classroom. For example, an AP Spanish course may be offered in a virtual classroom, while the AP math course is offered on site. The shortage of highly qualified teachers makes this a viable option for most school districts. Virtual schools are often supported by state or private agencies that enroll students to take much of their coursework online.

A virtual schooling system requires teachers to shift the way they think about instruction and to employ multiple technologies in creating a series of activities. A nationally recognized anatomy and physiology virtual school course conducted by Gail Wortman used videoconferencing several times a week (Davis & Niederhauser, 2007). Virtual schools often offer student support services, which may include desktop conferencing with teachers at a designated time. A recent survey conducted by Learning Circuits (2006) asked readers' opinion on the benefits of online learning synchronous events. The results show that 82% believe "conferences" are effective events. Using web conferencing software allows online instructors to present via video to a group of students. Students participate by camera or by chat depending on the web conferencing software.

Web 2.0

In the last few years, the explosion of accessible, free collaboration software on the Internet has enhanced opportunities for virtual classrooms. Web 2.0 represents a new, interactive trend that has emerged on the same old World Wide Web. This evolution of the web allows end-users to participate in sharing, networking, and creating online.

The savvy K–12 educator is no longer limited to one or the other collaborative tool for classroom instruction or for teaching and learning from a distance. Web 2.0 provides, at no cost, an array of open source software that can enrich and enhance an IVC collaboration project. Open source software applications are a result of a new way of doing business by software publishers, providing no-cost accessibility to early releases of their products.

Applications such as blogs, wikis, Moodle, Skype, Google Docs, and ePals represent a burgeoning trend in online interactive or production applications. For videoconferencing, these shared tools, used effectively, advance IVC projects, allowing students, teachers, and content providers to further develop collaborations through accessible project extensions.

Blogs are web pages where users can share thoughts, pictures, videos, and links. There are many websites that offer free blog hosting. Classroom teachers are using blogs to extend IVC lessons through reflection and sharing. For example, students keep a journal during the IVC project, chronicling experiences, discoveries, and resources.

Wikis, much the same as blogs, are web pages, or a collection of web pages, that allow modification by subscribed users. In other words, a wicki is a shared website. Teachers use wikis for such things as online collaboration and sharing best practices for videoconferencing.

Moodle, a free, open-source course management system, is used by IVC trainers to provide teachers with access to professional development. Captured IVC content can be added to a Moodle site through an RSS feed.

Skype provides free online telephony and supports desktop videoconferencing. While not as high quality as H.323 video and audio, it can satisfy a need for immediate one-to-one videoconferencing.

Google Docs, a free online document sharing site, supports student-to-student and classroom-to-classroom collaboration. With a free gmail account, students and teachers can post various types of documents so that multiple users can add and edit without the confusion of e-mailing documents back and forth.

ePals represents an example of a growing number of global networking sites, free to students and teachers around the world. ePals is an established preparation activity or extension activity for an IVC project.

These are just a few examples of how the evolution of the World Wide Web, from a passive tool to an interactive tool, has empowered distance learners who desire to extend or enhance their IVC collaborations from any place in the world.

Looking Ahead

Educational technology has progressed tremendously since the turn of the 21st century. Enrollment in K–12 distance education courses has more than doubled in recent years. There's no doubt K–12 learning environments will be significantly altered by the technologies developed in the last decade, technologies that will be improved upon in coming years. Teachers and students who embrace technology and digital delivery methods are limited only by access to equipment, a high-speed network infrastructure, and encouragement by innovative school administrators and government officials.

EXPLORE POSSIBILITIES

Nothing happens without a learning environment that encourages exploration of the possibilities (Vincent, 2003).

NCLB mandates may actually encourage virtual learning, as virtual learning programs clearly present a solution to the obstacles many school systems currently face in creating and sustaining equal learning opportunities. Emerging technologies and their application by early adopters have paved the way for a paradigm shift in K–12 education. As doors to virtual learning open wider and the new millennium unfolds, educators will need to face up to the challenge of incorporating this technology in the learning and teaching process. School systems must take into consideration the needs of today's students as well as the flexibility required to adapt to a rapidly changing technology environment and build or rebuild their educational technology plans accordingly.

To have a truly transformational impact on education, technology must become ubiquitous. It must always be available, mobile, and flexible. It must be intuitive, reliable, and user friendly to the point of being no more difficult to operate than a chalkboard, textbook, or overhead projector. It must be seamless and nearly invisible (Goldberg, 2002). IVC technology has come a long way toward achieving this kind of transparency.

As digital networks grow and bandwidth capacity increases, virtual learning will become more predominant in K–12 classrooms. It will be fundamental to the success of 21st-century teachers to create an interactive classroom that engages students by augmenting, with virtual learning technologies, the teacher's traditional classroom practices. As we strive to leave no child behind in this era of school budget cuts and uneven access to technology resources, IVC has an increasingly mainstream role to play. This is already evident in largely rural countries such as Australia and in states such as Alaska, where virtual learning has become a vital part of their educational systems. Virtual learning methods are quickly becoming a reasonable substitute that's used by alternative schools, homebound teachers, juvenile justice teachers, and a mixture of other nontraditional teaching environments.

It's always chancy to write about technology. By the time you read this book, many new opportunities and technological advances will already be on the market. We've nevertheless attempted to demonstrate that a plethora of affordable and accessible virtual learning modalities and programs are available to you, the K–12 classroom teacher, right now. Videoconferencing is one virtual learning option. Through IVC, you can enhance and enrich your curriculum by bringing to your classroom global and local educational resources on almost any topic, combining them with other Internet-based multimedia applications. These resources will benefit both your students, as participants in a competitive, technology-driven world, and you, as a lifelong learner.

There will always be a need for technology improvement as well as for time to train and adapt. In a perfect world, educational technology would be wireless, mobile, and accessible to everyone. It would be ubiquitous, intuitive, and familiar to all teachers and administrators. However, what the future holds for virtual learning technologies and programs remains to be seen—and it's unlikely to resemble that perfect world. It's up to you to take advantage, now, of the technology potentials that are already in place; and we hope that the information we've provided you in this book will encourage you to explore these virtual learning options. What you do with the possibilities, ideas, and options is up to you. If enough of you take them and use them and make them part of your classroom and instruction, school districts and the technology industry will follow your lead. You will make the difference.

The chapter that follows will provide you with a host of resources to get you started.

GLOBAL COMMUNITIES

The challenge becomes, how many magic links can we build between our students and the global community; between our school community and parents and the local community; and between our very isolated education professionals and the world of adult development and knowledge (November, 1997)?

Chapter 7

Resources for Videoconferencing

Community Partnerships

Interactive videoconferencing helps you bring rich educational resources directly to your classroom. It enables you to build partnerships with higher education and with cultural, scientific, business, and other community-based organizations. Every city, town, and village on the globe has something to offer learners, something to share with local, or even global, classrooms. If potential partners have access to videoconferencing technology and you also do, those resources are but an IVC connection away.

Most community organizations have an educational mission to fulfill. They also have limited outreach capacity. A trip to the other side of the state is expensive and time-consuming. Videoconferencing can bring, to classrooms around your state and beyond, symphonies, operas, theater productions, public television, historical tours, science demonstrations, and presentations by business and industry personnel. Videoconferencing can connect you and your students with higher education institutions where distance education technologies have been in place for nearly two decades. Through the implementation of IVC technology, new relationships and collaborations are formed within communities, across states, and around the world. Organizations and people rich in resources can work together to further both community and worldwide education goals.

KC3: KIDS CREATING COMMUNITY CONTENT, AN INTERNATIONAL IVC PROJECT

Bev Mattocks, Consultant
Center for Interactive Learning and Collaboration (CILC); Indianapolis, Indiana

Circling the globe from east to west, urban or rural, we each live in a unique community. What can we learn from our area, from its citizens, and from its natural resources?

KC3, a standards-based project, seeks to tap into the creative nature of students as they look at their community with new eyes and explore ways to share their findings with others using videoconferencing and technology as a resource. Students in Grades 6–12 create an engaging and dynamic videoconference content program about their community to be offered to classrooms internationally.

Student multimedia projects are presented to partner classes via IVC, captured via content server and then evaluated by independent education technologists (see Student Content Rubric in Appendix A). What a great way to combine a student collaborative project with community resources! See the KC3 website at http://kc3.cilc.org.

With the expansion and development of IVC technologies, community organizations as well as individuals—your potential partners—have become viable sources for education content and student engagement. Following are interviews with community-based partners who make use of virtual learning technologies to reach out and contribute to the educational wealth of their local schools and fulfill their own educational missions. They are but a few examples of how technology can link community resources to classrooms.

IVC fosters collaborations among community groups and schools.

A Professional Development Partnership

Interview with Claudia Wheatley, Director of Professional Development
Center for Interactive Learning and Collaboration (CILC); Indianapolis, Indiana

Camille Cole: Claudia, I understand you provide an extensive professional development program for educators and parents in Indiana via interactive videoconferencing. How did you get involved with IVC?

Claudia Wheatley: CILC conducted a needs assessment of schools throughout the state and received overwhelming input that IVC was needed as a vehicle to deliver ongoing professional development that could be used by all educators in the school community. CILC then came to me to help them build an infrastructure to provide professional development that aligns with best practices research, NCLB, and school improvement goals.

Camille: What did you discover during that process?

Claudia: That this is a way to do what we have wanted to do with professional development—to create a professional learning community. We found we could create opportunities for educators to learn without sacrificing quality student learning. Our programs are scheduled before and after school and during release and prep times. This makes it cost-effective and ensures that an initiative is implemented by the entire staff faster and more effectively. Everyone receives the training and, also, continued support via the technology.

Camille: How did you do that?

Claudia: After we determined content need for teachers, administrators, parents, and so on, we developed programming that had to be "just in time," "ongoing," and "best practice" (not "bleacher practice"). Today, we offer a leadership series, a best practices in action series, just in time information and training sessions, and opportunities for coaching and mentoring with highly trained specialists.

Camille: What does the program look like today?

Claudia: An example is a collegial series like "Writing Across the Curriculum," taught by Dr. Bailey from Indiana University, where teachers from across the state get to participate and work both with Dr. Bailey and with each other. It's one of our goals to connect those with great expertise with other people, on a regular basis, and to eliminate the need for travel in order to do that.

Camille: How do you actually interface with the schools?

Claudia: We have consultants working throughout the state who work directly with schools. We have a powerful vehicle with IVC—we develop collaborative programming from schools, the state Department of Education, education service centers, and teacher and principal associations; and we work with them to help them figure out how to disseminate programs more effectively.

Camille: What has been the benefit of working with an organization like CILC?

Claudia: Well, they're a nonprofit organization that had the opportunity to fine-tune the application of videoconferencing. Because of their expertise with the technology, we've been able to facilitate a marriage of content providers, those who need content, and the people who understand the technology.

Camille: What do you believe is the power behind this partnership?

Claudia: We're offering a service delivery model for the improvement of learning for all education stakeholders that is cost- and resource-effective.

A Student Partnership

Interview with Janine Lim, Instructional Technology Consultant, TWICE (Two Way Interactive Connections in Education), Berrien County Intermediate School District; Berrien Springs, Michigan

Camille Cole: Tell me about your experiences with collaborations and partnerships using interactive videoconferencing.

Janine Lim: When I hear the word collaboration, I think of kids-to-kids—that's the most powerful partnership we've seen.

Camille: How are you using that in Michigan?

Janine: We have the Michigan Collaborative, where students sign up for an "exchange" and get matched with other kids in parts of the state that are far away, different from their home communities. These exchanges last for 45 minutes. They spend the first part, for example, talking about their communities, and then they ask each other questions. One of my favorite examples is a session where one group had memorized that their city was 30 square miles in size. When asked, the small-town students didn't really know the official size of their community but could tell the other site that their town was four blocks long. They started asking each other questions like, "How many schools are there in your town?" and "How many students attend your school?" They really amazed each other, and the students from the small town asked the students from the large city, "Do you feel safe?" while the students from the large city asked the students in the small town, "Aren't you bored?"

Camille: What do you believe is the underlying power in the face-to-face connection that IVC provides?

Janine: Kids love talking to an audience other than their local school. They love seeing kids in other places. They love seeing the work that other kids do. In the end, I believe it motivates them to do better work. They get ideas. Creativity is contagious. If I'm asked how IVC affects student learning, I say, "Motivation."

Camille: What's been the biggest challenge for you as a practitioner?

Janine: I would say the reluctance of teachers. Getting them to the first good connection sometimes is a challenge. Things go wrong, and then we've lost them. The schools we've seen have the greatest success are those that have someone in the building to provide support and incentives, and those schools that have someone responsible for the equipment.

Camille: What is the underlying basis for success with videoconferencing in Michigan?

Janine: It's the strong partnership between our K–12 distance learning association, TWICE, and the school districts and education service organizations. It's the people who are coordinating distance education in the schools, who love learning and are willing to share expertise with those just getting started. It's the people who create great collaborative programs and share them willingly and freely with others.

A Nonprofit Partnership

Interview with Ruth Blankenbaker, Executive Director
Center for Interactive Learning and Collaboration (CILC); Indianapolis, Indiana

Kecia Ray: How long have you been an advocate of videoconferencing in K–12?

Ruth Blankenbaker: I've been driven to believe that access to information is a lifeline, and access to people is our soul. The Internet gives us access to information, but two-way interaction connects eye-to-eye and soul-to-soul.

Kecia: How did you become familiar with this tool?

Ruth: I was a technology director for Park Tudor School in Indianapolis for 11 years, and part of the technology deployment in that school was a fiber-optic network for voice video and data with a T-1 connection to the Internet. Because I believed that in 1992 information outside the hardbound text was a part of the driving vision required for 21st century education, it was important to have a technology infrastructure that allowed access to the world outside of the campus.

Kecia: What words of wisdom would you offer to our readers?

Ruth: Interactive video in the K–12 environment is still a relatively new technology. Inherent in its use, then, is the possibility for frustration and failure. Still, I would encourage educators to embrace its power, for they'll become paradigm pioneers, social entrepreneurs, and change agents who demonstrate with courage their desire to alter the future.

Kecia: Where do you see the application of videoconferencing technology in K–12 most effective?

Ruth: The challenge becomes crafting a use of the interactive technology that goes far beyond delivering classes by connecting learners to resources and places outside of their classroom. The fiber is a glass hallway that allows experts into our classroom, face-to-face. This is the energizing power that captures the minds of our kids.

Kecia: Where do you see videoconferencing technology in the classroom within the next five years?

Ruth: I think we'll get much closer to full-motion video in the classroom, which will take an infrastructure commitment from the schools. We'll also have learned the social skills necessary in a video environment. Access to experts will grow, and the teacher's role will morph from being the primary source of information to being a coordinator who knows where the experts are and how to reach them.

A Public School Partnership

Interview with Lisa Perez, Technology Resource Administrator
Department of e-Learning, Chicago Public Schools; Chicago, Illinois

Kecia Ray: How long have you been an advocate of videoconferencing in K–12?

Lisa Perez: Three years.

Kecia: How did you first come to use this tool for teaching?

Lisa: I was working in a high school librarian position. The IVC equipment was in the library but not used very much. I started advocating its use, and I was fortunate to have a progressive principal who supported me to the point of creating a position for distance learning.

Kecia: What pearls of wisdom about this technology would you like to share with our readers?

Lisa: Videoconferencing can highlight generational gaps. Teachers and administrators haven't grown up with this technology, and they don't always understand how to integrate the technology with learning. Young people, on the other hand, easily adapt to interactive videoconferencing, but they don't remain impressed by the technology itself for very long. It's our challenge to use videoconferencing to provide students with engaging, relevant learning experiences that are firmly based on our curricula and learning standards.

Kecia: Where do you see the application of videoconferencing in K–12 in the next five years?

Lisa: Similar to the issues with computers and the Internet, there'll be a widening "Videoconferencing Divide." Due to the fact that few teacher and administrator preparation programs address how to integrate videoconferencing technology into teaching, many school districts will lag behind in its implementation. Funding issues, coupled with a shortage of trained videoconferencing technical support persons, will compound these issues.

By contrast, other school districts will continue to mature in their use of videoconferencing. There will be more classes delivered via videoconferencing, promoting equity among schools. There will be more collaborative projects that join students from diverse geographic locations and allow them to work on a common, problem-based learning project. Internet2 will play an increasing role in creating quality of service and IP connectivity, allowing unprecedented and affordable access and opening the possibilities of sustained relationships between domestic and international students. Videoconferencing itself will become more ubiquitous, merging with computer software applications on the desktop or in large-room systems, depending on the specific communication needs.

Kecia: How do you feel videoconferencing affects the K–12 classroom?

Lisa: Videoconferencing enables students to access a much broader range of resources than could be accessed through traditional means. It fosters authentic, collaborative learning experiences, permitting students to interact with persons who may have significantly different viewpoints and perspectives. In the true spirit of constructivist learning, students can direct their own learning, due to the interactive, synchronous nature of the technology.

Since the technology involves visual as well as audio communication, it most closely replicates face-to-face interaction, creating a more natural learning experience. Since operation of the equipment involves a rather easy learning curve, even less experienced users can quickly adapt to the videoconferencing environment and concentrate more on the content. Once students and teachers become familiar with videoconferencing, it becomes a natural learning tool.

Content Providers

The Center for Interactive Learning and Collaboration (CILC) maintains a videoconference content provider directory (visit www.cilc.org and click on the Resources tab). This list, which is updated daily, includes detailed information on programs from these content providers. The following are examples of the programs available:

- Bronx Zoo/Wildlife Conservation Society: http://bronxzoo.com/distancelearning
- Carnegie Museum of Natural History: www.carnegiemnh.org
- Mote Marine Laboratory: www.seatrek.org
- Smithsonian American Art Museum: http://americanart.si.edu

Web Resources

Helpful websites to get you started...

ORGANIZATION	WEBSITE ADDRESS	DESCRIPTION
"How To" and Overviews		
Global SchoolNet	www.globalschoolnet.org	Elements of an effective IVC.
Video Cookbook, 4.1 Video Development Initiative	www.videnet.gatech.edu/cookbook/	Discussion of basic requirements and best practices for IVC, popular collaborative technologies, emerging technologies, network setup, advanced components, and management.
AT&T Knowledge Network Explorer	www.kn.att.com/wired/vidconf/intro.html	Detailed information about educational uses of IVC technology, including links to other videoconferencing teachers, librarians, and content providers.
CILC Professional Development Marketplace	www.cilc.org/c/education/professional_development_center.aspx	Professional development programs from nationally recognized educators delivered via IVC.
University of Idaho—Distance Learning at a Glance	www.uidaho.edu/eo/distglan.html	Thirteen online guides for every area of distance learning.
Collaborative Projects		
AT&T Knowledge Network Collaboration Collage	www.kn.att.com/wired/vidconf/ed1vidconf.html	An e-mail list you can join to find other teachers interested in collaborative projects.
TWICE	www.twice.cc/projects.html	Collaborative projects for national and international exchange.
CILC Collaboration Center	www.cilc.org/c/community/collaboration_center.aspx	A national database of current collaborative project ideas. To find classroom partners, you can browse postings from other teachers, search by topic and grade, and post your own ideas.
White Plains Middle School's Global Run Project	http://globalrunproject.org	An annual global project that connects classes to work on a yearlong project that benefits the planet.

ORGANIZATION	WEBSITE ADDRESS	DESCRIPTION
Searchable Databases		
AT&T Knowledge Network Explorer	www.kn.att.com/wired/vidconf/directory.html	Videoconference sites. Searchable by state or country.
St. Joseph's University International Videoconferencing List	www.sju.edu/ims//vc_list1.htm	Videoconference sites. Searchable by state or country.
TWICE	www.twice.cc/fieldtrips.html	Searchable by keywords or provider; teacher ratings available.
CILC	www.cilc.org/education/content_provider_programs.aspx	Searchable by keywords or provider; teacher ratings available.
Educational Enterprise Zone (EEZ)	www.nyiteez.org/providers.htm	List of content providers.
IVC Blogs of Interest		
Avon, Ohio's Interactive Distance Learning Blog	http://avonoh-ivc.blogspot.com	This blog is a diary of the NORT2H Consortium of Northeast Ohio, a consortium of schools using video-conferencing in a blended model of mutiple technologies to enhance student learning.
The Wired Classroom	http://csdtechpd.wordpress.com	Sponsored by the Virtual Learning Center at Cooperating School Districts in St. Louis, MO, the materials on this blog help teachers use their wired classrooms to the fullest advantage.
Videoconferencing Out on a Lim	http://vcoutonalim.org	Everyday classroom teachers share their stories about how they are utilizing web 2.0 tools and videoconferencing in their classrooms. Find links here to more IVC resources.
VC Rox	www.edlink12.net/vcrox/	Sponsored by Roxanne Glaser, a distance learning specialist.
Videoconference Tips and Techniques	http://videoconference.edublogs.org	Great ideas for better videoconferences from Carol Skyring, Learntel, Australia

ORGANIZATION	WEBSITE ADDRESS	DESCRIPTION
Vendor Information		
VTEL	www.vtel.com	IVC hardware, software, and planning information.
TANDBERG	www.tandberg.com	IVC hardware, infrastructure, and support programs.
Polycom	www.polycom.com/home/	IVC hardware information.
LifeSize	http://lifesize.com	IVC hardware information.
Online Articles		
A History of Videoconferencing	http://myhome.hanafos.com/ ~soonjp/vchx.html	Timeline of IVC development 1956–2002.
Pelegroup.net Partnership for Emerging Learning Environments	www.pelegroup.net/resources/ index.html	A collection of articles about IVC, Internet2, virtual reality, and other emerging technologies.
Bibliography of Online Articles about IVC	www.twice.cc/rbib.html	Everything you ever wanted to know about IVC in education.
Miscellaneous		
Copyright Management Center	www.copyright.iupui.edu	Detailed information on copyright and fair use issues in the classroom.
Internet2 K–20 Initiative	http://k20.Internet2.edu/index.php	Internet2 clearinghouse that provides information about new technology applications and middle-ware, and links content providers and educational organizations across the United States. Includes an Internet2 detective to determine if your school is connected to Internet2.

Tools and Templates

- Teacher Evaluation for IVC Lesson
- Student Evaluation for IVC Lesson
- Long-Term Virtual Learning Planning Chart
- Videoconference Script/Storyboard Template
- Videoconference Lesson Plan Template
- Content Provider Follow-Up Form
- Videoconference Log
- Videoconferencing Equipment and Line Inventory
- Fair Use Checklist
- Student Content Rubric

Teacher Evaluation for IVC Lesson

GRADE LEVEL: _____

SUBJECT: _____

DATE OF IVC: _____

TIME OF IVC: _____

TYPE OF IVC EQUIPMENT AT REMOTE SITE: _____

Rate the following statements from 4 (strongly agree) to 1 (strongly disagree).

STATEMENT	RATING			
This is the first videoconference this class has participated in this year.	④	③	②	①
The videoconference was an enhancement to the planned lesson.	④	③	②	①
The videoconference was enrichment to the planned lesson.	④	③	②	①
The videoconference met the expectations of the lesson objective.	④	③	②	①
The students were engaged throughout the entire videoconference.	④	③	②	①
Pre-videoconference activities supported the content delivered.	④	③	②	①
Activities within the context of the videoconference supported the lesson objective.	④	③	②	①
Post-videoconference activities supported the content delivered.	④	③	②	①
Assessment indicated students retained information presented within the context of the videoconference.	④	③	②	①
Summative evaluations of unit objectives indicate students are receptive to content delivered via videoconference.	④	③	②	①
More than one school connected through the videoconference for this lesson.	④	③	②	①
There was interaction among the multiple points of the videoconference.	④	③	②	①
The facilitator was effective in managing the agenda for the videoconference.	④	③	②	①
The content provider was effective in delivering appropriate and related content to enhance or enrich the lesson objective.	④	③	②	①

Student Evaluation for IVC Lesson

GRADE LEVEL: _____

SUBJECT: _____

DATE OF IVC: _____

TIME OF IVC: _____

TYPE OF IVC EQUIPMENT AT REMOTE SITE: _____

Rate the following statements from 4 (strongly agree) to 1 (strongly disagree).

STATEMENT	RATING			
This is the first videoconference I have participated in this year.	④	③	②	①
The videoconference was in addition to the lesson my teacher was teaching.	④	③	②	①
The videoconference was a part of the lesson my teacher was teaching.	④	③	②	①
The presenter was easy to understand and communicate with during the videoconference.	④	③	②	①
The presenter offered a question/answer time at the end of the videoconference.	④	③	②	①
Pre-videoconference activities supported the content delivered.	④	③	②	①
Activities during the videoconference supported the lesson we were doing in class.	④	③	②	①
Post-videoconference activities supported the content delivered.	④	③	②	①
I will use information learned from the videoconference when I take the test on this lesson.	④	③	②	①
I learned something from the videoconference that I did not know before.	④	③	②	①
Everyone in my class paid attention to the presenter during the videoconference.	④	③	②	①
More than one classroom participated in the videoconference.	④	③	②	①
My teacher was in charge of the videoconference.	④	③	②	①
The remote location was in charge of the videoconference.	④	③	②	①

Long-Term Virtual Learning Planning Chart

Name of Content Provider (include URL)	Topic/ Objective	Contact Person E-mail and Phone	Anticipated Date(s) of IVC	Cost	Notes	ISDN or IP Numbers Needed to Place Call

Subject: _____   Unit Objective: _____

Videoconference Script/Storyboard Template

IVC Title:	Originating Location:	Remote Location:
Date:	Time:	Time Frame (length of time allocated):
Facilitator:		Tech Support:

SEGMENT	LESSON OBJECTIVE	MEDIA	EQUIPMENT	DIALOGUE
Length of Each Segment	What You Plan to Accomplish	Type of Media to be Used	IVC Equipment/ Peripheral to Be Used	Insert Conversational Cues

Videoconference Lesson Plan Template

LESSON BY: _____

SUBJECT AREA: _____

GRADE LEVEL: _____

NETS•S ADDRESSED: _____

CONTENT STANDARDS ADDRESSED: _____
*This section should indicate the alignment of lesson objectives
with state and national benchmarks and standards.*

DURATION *(e.g., three to four class periods)*: _____

VOCABULARY:
List words to be introduced through this lesson.

Unit Goal:

Unit Objectives
After completing this lesson, the students will be able to:

Prior Knowledge Required
Students should have an understanding of:

(Continued)

Pre-Conference Activities

Activity 1

INSTRUCTIONAL OBJECTIVE:

MATERIALS:

PROCEDURE:

EVALUATION:

Activity 2

INSTRUCTIONAL OBJECTIVE:

MATERIALS:

PROCEDURE:

EVALUATION:

Preparation for Videoconference

✓ Overview of behavior expected during videoconference

✓ Sign noting school name and location

✓ Student questions to be asked (write them out and review with class the procedure for interaction)

Videoconference

TOPIC:

CONTENT PROVIDER (OR REMOTE SITE):

INTRODUCTION:

ACTIVITY OR PRESENTATION:

QUESTION/ANSWER OR DISCUSSION (10–15 MINUTES):

Provide directions for how this interaction will take place. For example, who will ask the leading question, who will respond, how long each student will have to ask or respond to a question, etc.

Post-Conference Activities

Follow-Up Activity

INSTRUCTIONAL OBJECTIVE:

MATERIALS:

PROCEDURE:

EVALUATION:

Content Provider Follow-Up Form

NAME OF CONTENT PROVIDER:

CONTACT PERSON:	PHONE:

E-MAIL:

TOPICS OF INTEREST:

CONNECTION TO CURRICULUM:

LOCATION OF CONTENT PROVIDER:

TIME ZONE:	ANTICIPATED DATE OF IVC(S):

FEE:	P.O. NUMBER (IF REQUIRED):

OTHER COSTS:	FAILURE-TO-CONNECT POLICY:

MATERIALS PROVIDED TO CLASS:

FORMAT/ABBREVIATED AGENDA:

Videoconference Log

SCHOOL/CONTENT PROVIDER:	LESSON OBJECTIVE:	
DATE SCHEDULED	TIME (note time zone)	REMOTE CONTACT INFORMATION	ISDN/IP NUMBER

SCHOOL/CONTENT PROVIDER:	LESSON OBJECTIVE:	
DATE SCHEDULED	TIME (note time zone)	REMOTE CONTACT INFORMATION	ISDN/IP NUMBER

SCHOOL/CONTENT PROVIDER:	LESSON OBJECTIVE:	
DATE SCHEDULED	TIME (note time zone)	REMOTE CONTACT INFORMATION	ISDN/IP NUMBER

Videoconferencing Equipment and Line Inventory

DATE: _____

SCHOOL: _____

PHONE: _____   FAX: _____

PRINCIPAL: _____   E-MAIL: _____

TEACHER: _____   E-MAIL: _____

TECHNICIAN: _____   E-MAIL: _____

DISTRICT CONTACT: _____   E-MAIL: _____

STATE CONTACT: _____   E-MAIL: _____

EQUIPMENT INVENTORY	
HARDWARE	**SERIAL NUMBER**
Codec	
Camera	
NT1	
Cart	
Monitor	
Peripherals (list below)	

LINE INVENTORY		
LINE	**LOCATION IN ROOM**	**NUMBER**
ISDN Line 1		
ISDN Line 2		
ISDN Line 3		

Fair Use Checklist

Is It Really Fair Use?

✓ *Check all that apply*

FAIR USE	NOT FAIR USE
How will the copyrighted work be used?	
☐ Teaching	☐ Commercial activity
☐ Research	☐ For profit
☐ Nonprofit education	☐ For entertainment
☐ Restricted access (e.g., students)	☐ Without following copyright laws
☐ New use or to add value to work (author credited)	☐ Without crediting author
What type of copyrighted work will be used?	
☐ Published work	☐ Unpublished work
☐ Fact- or nonfiction-based work	☐ Creative work (art, music, films, plays, etc.)
☐ Work keyed to educational objectives	☐ Works of fiction
How much copyrighted work will be used?	
☐ Small amount, appropriate for educational purposes	☐ Large amount, significant to the entire work
How will using the copyrighted work affect the market for the work?	
☐ No adverse effect; user owns lawfully acquired or purchased copy of original work	☐ Adverse effect if made openly accessible on the Internet or other public forum
☐ One or few copies made with no significant effect on market for copyrighted work	☐ Could reduce sales of copyrighted work if numerous copies made
☐ No licensing mechanism	☐ Adverse effect if affordable license fee available for using work isn't paid

Adapted from documents prepared by the Copyright Management Center, Indiana University, Purdue University Indianapolis

Student Content Rubric

This is a sample rubric for evaluating student-generated content being delivered via IVC.

SCORING RUBRIC: STUDENT CONTENT PROGRAM	
1 = Weak 2 = Fair 3 = Good 4 = Very Good 5 = Outstanding	

COMPONENT	CRITERIA
Topic	• Presentation aligns with the identified grade level • Topic has cultural/community significance • Topic lends itself to building greater understanding of our diversity
Content Knowledge	• Topic content is clear and meets presentation objectives • Content is educational; suitable to grade level participants • Demonstrates full knowledge of the topic; explains and elaborates
Research	• Evidence of research on topic from more than one source
Presentation Strategies	• Information presented in logical, interesting sequence that audience can follow • Age-appropriate questioning and response skills • Student properly generates questions from the audience • Presentation incorporates interactive strategies/activities
Audience Engagement	• Establishes rapport with the audience before and during the presentation • Audience participation encouraged • Variety of engagement techniques
Delivery	• Enthusiastic, expressive • Voice quality/clarity/tone • Eye/camera contact • Articulate, comfortable communicating with the audience • Program stays within time limits (begins and ends on time)

(Continued)

Student Content Rubric *(Continued)*

COMPONENT	CRITERIA
IVC Setting	• Acceptable transmission delay • Visually appealing • Quiet auditory background • Works to minimize distractions
Creativity	• Original, inventive • Unique, fresh • Captures audience attention • Variety and blend of experiences for the audience
Visuals/Media/Graphics	• Effectively reinforces or presents material/concepts • Appealing; makes presentation more interesting • Add to the presentation in a genuine way, not used excessively • Varied and appropriate
Presentation Team	• Works well as a group • Holds audience interest/attention throughout • Uses technology effectively
Additional Materials Optional *(bonus points awarded)*	• Supports presentation objectives • Additional resources available for audience participants • Pre- and/or post-videoconference materials: activities, websites, wikis, blogs, reading material, vocabulary

Rubric courtesy of the Center for Interactive Learning and Collaboration.

Sample IVC Lessons

Elementary IVC Unit
The Life and Times of a Lakota Sioux

LESSON BY: Frances Gary, Lakeside Park Elementary School

SUBJECT AREA: Social Studies

GRADE LEVEL: 4–5

NETS•S ADDRESSED: 3, 4

CONTENT STANDARDS ADDRESSED:

Social Sciences

1.01   Understand the diversity of human cultures.

1.03   Recognize the contributions of people of various ethnic, racial, religious, and socioeconomic groups to the development of civilizations.

4.1.02 Explore similarities and differences in how groups, societies, and cultures address similar human needs and concerns.

4.2.07 Write narrative accounts with developed characters, setting, and plot.

4.2.08 Investigate content-specific topics to gather information and write.

5.10   Recognize American territorial expansions and its effects on relations with European powers and Native Americans.

5.11   Understand sectional differences brought on by the Western movement, expansion of slavery, and emerging industrialization.

DURATION: Four lessons

VOCABULARY:

Words introduced through this lesson:
Lakota
Sioux
Crazy Horse
Sitting Bull
Battle of Little Bighorn
reservation
teepee
George Custer
buffalo or calendar robe
Indian picture writing

Words taught after the videoconference based on student interest:
D-day
Normandy
Pearl Harbor
Hitler
atomic bomb

Unit Goal

Learn about the way of life of Native American Lakota and the conflict between Lakota Sioux and settlers.

Unit Objectives

After completing this lesson, students will be able to:

- Write their own stories of the life of a young Lakota boy living in South Dakota
- Complete an Indian buffalo-skin story using Indian picture writing

Prior Knowledge Required

Students should understand that the Lakota Sioux were a well-known group of Native Americans who lived in a region of the Great Plains that now includes Minnesota, Wyoming, North Dakota, and South Dakota. They should be able to locate this region on a map. The Black Hills mountains of South Dakota were the best winter hunting grounds of the Lakota. When gold was discovered there in 1874, the government ordered the land be given up, and settlers quickly began arriving.

The Lakota Sioux were skilled horsemen, and they depended on buffalo for their way of life. The coming of the railroad and settlers to their hunting grounds changed the way of life of the Lakota and destroyed the buffalo herds.

Crazy Horse and Sitting Bull are two famous Lakota chiefs. They were attacked in 1876 by General George Custer at the Battle of Little Bighorn in Montana. Because in the battle the Lakota killed Custer and all of his troops, it became known as Custer's Last Stand.

Pre-Conference Activities

Activity 1 (Day 1)

ACTIVITY OBJECTIVE
Learn about the Lakota way of life and the importance of the buffalo.

MATERIALS
Video: Great Indian Nations, by Questar Home Video

Books: *If You Lived With the Sioux Indians*, by Ann McGovern

PROCEDURE
Watch the video Great Indian Nations. Introduce the book *If You Lived With the Sioux Indians*. Assign each student a topic from the book to read and illustrate.

EVALUATION
Have students write a brief summary of the content and present it orally to the rest of the class, using their illustration in their presentation. One student presentation will include using a large map to locate and show the home of the Sioux.

Activity 2 (Day 2)

ACTIVITY OBJECTIVE
Understand why a conflict arose between the Lakota, the U.S. Army, and the settlers.

MATERIALS
Regions Adventures in Time and Place (classroom textbook)

The Sioux: A First American Book, by Virginia Driving Hawk Sneve

"The Buffalo Go," by Old Lady Horse. Excerpted from *American Indian Mythology*, by Alice Marriott and Carol Rachlin

A Boy Called Slow: The True Story of Sitting Bull, by Joseph Bruchac

Buffalo Hunt, by Russell Freedman

End of the Trail, an NBC Time Travel Documentary narrated by Walter Brennan, produced by Universal International, 1965

PROCEDURE
Have students listen to excerpts from Russell Freedman's *Buffalo Hunt* and "The Buffalo Go," and then read "The Lakota of the Plains" from their social studies textbook, *Regions Adventures in Time and Place*.

EVALUATION
Have each student write a short paragraph about the importance of the buffalo to the Lakota and list at least three reasons why the Lakota were forced onto a reservation.

Preparation for Videoconference

✓ Prepare students for interactive and behavioral expectations during the videoconference.

✓ Ask students to create a site-location sign.

✓ Have students watch the video End of the Trail.

Videoconference

TOPIC
The Life and Times of a Lakota Sioux

CONTENT PROVIDER
Black Hills Smart Center, South Dakota.

PRESENTER
Chief David Bald Eagle

CONTACT PERSON
Elaine Shuck, eshuck@tie.net

INTRODUCTION
Chief David Bald Eagle talks about his life growing up in South Dakota and the stories he heard from his family, including the Battle of Little Bighorn, where his grandfather fought. He also served in World War II and was a survivor of Normandy Beach. Later, he became a professional baseball player.

QUESTION/ANSWER OR DISCUSSION
Students take notes on the videoconference, and as they're listening they write down questions that interest them. When the opportunity is given to ask questions, students raise their hands, and the camera is focused on the child whose turn it is to ask questions. What I noticed about fourth-graders in this videoconference was that after the confer-ence was over, they really asked good questions. What was D-day? What does the D stand for? What was Normandy? These questions led to much follow-up discussion and further learning related to World War II, Pearl Harbor, Normandy Beach, and the atomic bomb.

Post-Conference Activity

Write a first-person narrative as young David Bald Eagle growing up in South Dakota on an Indian reservation. The fictional narrative will be the basis for an art project, where the story will be translated into Indian picture writing and drawn on a "buffalo" calendar robe (distressed brown paper grocery bag).

ACTIVITY OBJECTIVES
* Investigate content-specific topics to gather information and write.
* Write narrative accounts, with developed characters, setting, and plot.

MATERIALS
Indian Two Feet and His Horse, by Margaret Friskey

Writing material

Indian pictographs for each child

Distressed brown paper bag (A large brown grocery bag can be made distressed by crumpling and uncrumpling it 100 times. This needs to be done before the art project. Each student will need only half a bag.)

Crayons or markers

PROCEDURE

The teacher will read *Indian Two Feet and His Horse*. The story follows the simple tale of a young brave as he tries to catch a horse. The teacher and students will brainstorm to create a bank of words that would be appropriate for a story. These are written on the board so that the students easily spell the words. The students will then write a brief narrative (about one page) of a day in the life of young David Bald Eagle. Their settings and characters are limited to the related pictographs they have available to use. After their stories have been written in English and shared orally, they will draw the pictographs, on the "buffalo" robe, to retell their story.

EVALUATION

The stories written in English will be graded for content, punctuation, and grammar.

Additional Resources

BOOKS

My Prairie Year, by Brett Harvey, 1986

Turquoise Boy, A Navajo Legend, by Terri Cohlene, 1990

Annie and the Old One, by Miska Miles, 1971

Thirteen Moons on Turtle's Back, A Native Year of Moons, by Joseph Bruchac and Jonathan London, 1992

Sadako and the Thousand Paper Cranes, by Eleanor Coerr, 1977

Children of the Wild West, by Russell Freedman, 1983

Indian Two Feet and His Eagle Feather, by Margaret Friskey, 1967

The Life and Times of a Lakota Sioux—Unit Script

IVC Title: The Life and Times of a Lakota Sioux	Originating Location: Lakeside Park Elementary School	Remote Location: Black Hills Smart Center
Date: Monday	Time: 9–10 a.m.	Time Frame (length of time allocated): 1 hour
Facilitator: Elaine Shuck	Tech Support: John Brown	

SEGMENT	LESSON OBJECTIVE	MEDIA	EQUIPMENT	DIALOGUE
Length of Each Segment	What You Plan to Accomplish	Type of Media to Be Used	IVC Equipment/ Peripheral to Be Used	Insert Conversational Cues
9:00–9:30	Introduce Chief David Bald Eagle; he tells his story	Camera one, head shot	Document camera	Chief Bald Eagle talks and students take notes in preparation for asking questions during the second segment.
9:30–10:30	Question/Answer/ Discussion	Camera one, head shots	Document camera	Students raise hands and wait for camera to come to them to ask prepared questions of Chief Bald Eagle.

Middle School IVC Unit
The Geology of Carving

SUBJECT AREA: Science/Geology

GRADE LEVEL: 5–6

NET•S ADDRESSED: 3–5

CONTENT STANDARDS ADDRESSED:

Score Science, sixth-grade content standards:
http://scorescience.humboldt.k12.ca.us/fast/teachers/content/6th.htm

Investigation and Experimentation

7. **Scientific progress is made by asking meaningful questions and conducting careful investigations.** As a basis for understanding this concept, and to address the content of the other three strands, students should develop their own questions and perform investigations. Students will:

   a. develop a hypothesis.

   b. select and use appropriate tools and technology (including calculators, computers, balances, spring scales, microscopes, and binoculars) to perform tests, collect data, and display data.

   c. construct appropriate graphs from data and develop qualitative statements about the relationships between variables.

   d. communicate the steps and results from an investigation in written reports and verbal presentations.

   e. recognize whether evidence is consistent with a proposed explanation.

   f. read a topographic map and a geologic map for evidence provided on the maps, and construct and interpret a simple scale map.

   g. interpret events by sequence and time from natural phenomena (e.g., relative ages of rocks and intrusions).

   h. identify changes in natural phenomena over time without manipulating the phenomena (e.g., a tree limb, a grove of trees, a stream, a hillslope).

DURATION: Three lessons

VOCABULARY:

Words introduced through this lesson:
mineral
rock cycle
igneous rock
crystal
sedimentary rock
metamorphic rock
terrain
erosion
weathering

Words taught after the videoconference based on student interest:
granitic
sculpture
shrine

Unit Goal

Students will recognize the relationship between natural materials and technologies.

Unit Objectives

Working in cooperative groups, each group will identify three (6"–9" in diameter) rock samples indigenous to their states.

Prior Knowledge Required

Students should have knowledge of Mount Rushmore: its history, its location. Students should also have knowledge of at least one other monumental statue, preferably one located in their own state.

Mount Rushmore features the faces of four American presidents: George Washington, Thomas Jefferson, Theodore Roosevelt, and Abraham Lincoln. Carved into South Dakota's Black Hills, it's the world's most massive mountain carving. Each face is 60 feet tall and 500 feet above the ground.

The sculptor, Gutzon Borglum, began drilling into the 5,725-foot mountain in 1927. The carving would not be complete for another 14 years.

The Black Hills are also known as the Island in the Prairie, an island of granite mountains surrounded by a sea of prairie grasses and a diverse plant and animal kingdom.

Pre-Conference Activity

Activity 1 (Day 1)

ACTIVITY OBJECTIVE
Learn how different types of rocks respond to carving and the technologies used for carving.

MATERIALS
Rock samples, carving tools, water, freezer, chart paper, colored pencils, cameras (optional)

PROCEDURE
The teacher will review igneous, sedimentary, and metamorphic rocks, as well as weathering and erosion. In groups, students will select technologies to use to carve an outline of their state into the rock sample. Students will then pour water into the furrow of their best-carved sample and allow the water to freeze. Repeat this step at least two times prior to the videoconference.

Throughout the activity, students will chart the type of sample used, the type of technology attempted, and the time it takes to establish the carving, and they will include a description of their attempt. Each group should also note on the chart the results of freezing the sample. Students may elect to archive the process by taking photographs of their samples during each interval.

EVALUATION
During the videoconference, each group will present its chart to the geologist.

Preparation for Videoconference

✓ Remind each group to bring its project sheet and rock carving to the videoconference.

✓ Have students prepare site-location signs.

Videoconference

TOPIC
The Geology of Carving

PRESENTERS
Students

ACTIVITIES
Teachers will set up signs giving the location of the videoconference, establish connection, and introduce cooperative groups during the videoconference. Each group within the class should select a speaker to speak on its behalf. The groups will share their findings with the audience, and the geologist will elaborate on the significance of these findings as related to earth science. Discussion of charts will ensue, and the geologist will answer any questions related to the project. At the conclusion of the videoconference, the curator will share with the audience technologies used in creating the monument. The videoconference will close with each class sharing its carved sample with the audience.

Additional Resources

BOOKS
Mount Rushmore (Building History Series), by Judith Janda Presnall

Mount Rushmore (Building America), by Craig A. Doherty, Katherine M. Doherty, and Bruce S. Glassman (Eds.)

Carving a Dream, by Robb DeWall. A photo history of Crazy Horse Memorial and the Ziolkowski family, a year-to-year chronology of the progress, and dramatic photos Korczak Ziolkowski took of his sculpture.

GEOLOGY WEBSITES
The Geology of Mount Rushmore: www.aqd.nps.gov/grd/parks/moru/

Geological Society Teacher Resources: www.geosociety.org/educate/

U.S. Geology Survey: www.usgs.gov

BACKGROUND WEBSITES
History of Mount Rushmore:
    www.travelsd.com/parks/rushmore/history.htm
    www.nps.gov/moru/

South Dakota:
    kidzone.travelsd.com/history/past.asp
    www.mediasd.com/facts/crazyhorse.asp

Crazy Horse Memorial:
    Travel SD.com: http://www.travelsd.com/parks/crazyhorse/ (*includes Webcam*)
    www.crazyhorse.org/story/future.shtml
    www.cnn.com/TRAVEL/NEWS/9805/12/crazy.horse/ (*contains QuickTime clips*)
    http://home.ptd.net/~mmzjr/crazyhrs.htm

VIDEO
Monumental Statues. Interviews with people who worked on Mount Rushmore and the massive Crazy Horse sculpture reveal the attraction and danger of fashioning the largest statues on earth. 50 minutes.

Post-Conference Activities

Follow-Up Activities

INSTRUCTIONAL OBJECTIVE
* Students will be able to describe relationship between geological conditions and success or failure of monumental carvings.

* Students will be able to use multimedia technologies to display project results.

MATERIALS
Writing materials, computer lab, multimedia software, art supplies

PROCEDURE/ACTIVITIES
* Write a short paper on the relationship between the rock sample and the success or failure of the technologies attempted.

* Compare and contrast technologies used to create Mount Rushmore to technologies used to create the Crazy Horse Monument.

* Create a digital presentation representing the project.

* Create an iMovie retelling the project.

* Create a poster demonstrating the relationship between the project the group completed and the building of the monument.

Evaluation: *The Geology of Carving*

NAME OF GROUP:

GROUP MEMBERS:

1. _____   3. _____

2. _____   4. _____

Type of Rock Sample	Type of Technology	Time Elapsed from Beginning to End of Carving	Results of Freezing*

*Only one of the three samples will be tested by freezing water.

The Geology of Carving—Unit Script

IVC Title:	Originating Location:	Remote Location:
The Geology of Carving	Mount Rushmore	Smith Middle School, Hopkins Middle School, Mountain Middle School

Date:	Time:	Time Frame (length of time allocated):
March 31, 2008	12:30–2:00 CST	90 minutes

Facilitator:	Tech Support:
Marci	University of Tennessee

SEGMENT	LESSON OBJECTIVE	MEDIA	EQUIPMENT	DIALOGUE
Length of Each Segment	What You Plan to Accomplish	Type of Media to Be Used	IVC Equipment/ Peripheral to Be Used	Insert Conversational Cues
12:30–12:55	Introductions and roll call	Camera image	Camera one	Facilitator calls on each site in turn and students introduce themselves. Geology expert is introduced.
12:55–1:05	Set the stage with music	Music CD	PC-based CD player	Theme from *Dances With Wolves*.
1:05–1:15	Welcome; opening remarks; review details of presentation	Video	Camera one; document camera	• Discuss technologies used to create monuments in South Dakota. • Explore geological elements of monuments in South Dakota.
1:15–1:17	Introduction of speakers	Video	Camera one; document camera	Facilitator introduces geology expert and displays, on document camera, picture of Mount Rushmore.

(Continued)

The Geology of Carving—Unit Script *(Continued)*

SEGMENT	LESSON OBJECTIVE	MEDIA	EQUIPMENT	DIALOGUE
Length of Each Segment	**What You Plan to Accomplish**	**Type of Media to Be Used**	**IVC Equipment/ Peripheral to Be Used**	**Insert Conversational Cues**
1:17–1:25	Introduction of concept of a geology expert and how that field relates to lesson	Video	Camera one	Geologist describes what he does for a living and how geology relates to the lesson at hand.
1:25–1:45	Students interact with geologist	Video	Camera one; document camera	Each group shares findings from projects.
1:45–1:50	Getting aquainted with Mount Rushmore expert	Video	Camera one	Facilitator introduces Mount Rushmore expert, who discusses technologies used to create monument. He talks about why the type of rock is significant to the successful completion of the monument.
1:50–2:00	Sharing projects and conclusions	Video	Camera one; document camera	• Student groups share carved samples • Discussion/ Comments • Closing remarks • Disconnect call

High School IVC Unit
AP Physics

LESSON BY: Brian Hanna, Newport High School

SUBJECT AREA: Math

GRADE LEVEL: 11–12

NETS•S ADDRESSED: 3, 6

CONTENT STANDARDS ADDRESSED (OREGON):

1. **Calculations and Estimations**

    A. Use computation, estimation, and mathematical properties to solve problems; use estimation to check the reasonableness of results, including those obtained by technology.

2. **Statistics and Probability**

    A. Use experimental or theoretical probability to represent and interpret situations or problems involving uncertainty.

3. **Algebraic Relationships**

    A. Simplify expressions and solve equations involving advanced functions.

    B. Understand and analyze the behavior of advanced functions.

    C. Model situations and solve problems using a variety of functions.

4. **Mathematical Problem Solving**

    A. Understand and formulate problems; select or provide relevant information; use mathematical concepts, models, and representations.

    B. Consider and choose among various strategies, algorithms, models, and concepts to devise and carry out solutions.

    C. Represent and communicate reasoning processes, solutions, ideas, and conclusions; use correct mathematical terminology, symbols, and notation.

DURATION: Three to four class periods

VOCABULARY:

Atwood machine
Negligible mass and/or friction

Unit Goal

Students will understand and be able to use Newton's Second Law of Motion to analyze multiple-object motion.

Unit Objective

After completing this unit, students will be able to use Newton's Second Law of Motion to analyze connected objects undergoing equivalent or opposite acceleration (neglecting friction).

Prior Knowledge Required

Students should have a knowledge of Newton's Laws of Motion and the form of Newton's Second Law written as:

$$\Sigma\, Forces = mass \times acceleration$$

Students should be familiar with this equation and its application in one dimension.

Students should know that the value of g used in class is 9.8 m/s^2.

Pre-Conference Activities

Not applicable for daily class.

Preparation for Videoconference

✓ Students are trained in use of the videoconferencing modality at the beginning of the term, including interaction protocol, teacher expectations, and directions for accessing class materials and assignments.

Lesson Notes

DAILY QUIZ
A large, light ball falls from a rooftop. Because of air resistance, however, its acceleration due to gravity is only 7.5 m/s^2. Determine the time required for it to reach the ground if the roof to ground distance is 1.0 m.

ANSWER
Using the previously introduced (prior lesson) equation d = 0.5×a×t^2, students will solve for t and determine the time to be 1.6 s. The following equation for time will be used in the practical application problem:

$$t = \sqrt{\frac{2 \times d}{a}}$$

DEMONSTRATION
The setup for the demonstration of Atwood's machine consists of a single pulley system about 50 cm above a level surface and various hooked weights or weight hangars in increments of 20 g with a string between them.

The demonstration and discussion begins with equal weights on both sides of the pulley and the analysis of the forces acting on both weights. Weights are then added to one side to initiate acceleration. An analysis of forces leads to the equation for the acceleration.

$$a = \frac{m_1 - m_2}{m_1 + m_2}$$

APPLICATION

As each part of the problem is read, I use two small dolls and a small cup of nails to illustrate. The practical application problem consists of the following:

> Buzz and Woody's Construction Company is working on a building. To assist in hauling equipment, a pulley system is installed to move tools and supplies up and down. Buzz (weight = 800 Newtons) and Woody (weight = 600 N) are 10 m up on a platform when they begin hauling up a crate (weight = 700 N) of nails (weight = 200 N). Unfortunately, just as they begin pulling the crate up, Buzz finds that he has inadvertently wrapped the rope around their legs, bends down to untie them, and knocks them both over the edge. After hitting the ground, Buzz gets his legs free and rolls away from Woody. The loss of weight at the ground end sends Woody back up, still tied to the rope, and the crate of nails crashing down. When the crate of nails hits the ground, the nails spill out and Woody again plummets to the earth. Stunned, but not yet unconscious, Woody gets free and tries to roll away. Before doing so, the empty crate smacks him on the head, knocking Woody out cold. Assume the mass of the rope and pulley, as well as any friction, is negligible. Determine the minimum amount of time necessary for this tragic event to occur.

Post-Conference Activities

Not applicable for daily class.

AP Physics—Unit Script

IVC Title: AP Physics	Originating Location: Newport High School	Remote Locations: Waldport High, Taft High, Oakridge High
Date: M–F	Time: 7:30 a.m.	Time Frame (length of time allocated): 45 minutes
Facilitator: Brian Hanna		Tech Support: Salem (NOC)

SEGMENT	LESSON OBJECTIVE	MEDIA	EQUIPMENT	DIALOGUE
Length of Each Segment	What You Plan to Accomplish	Type of Media to Be Used	IVC Equipment/ Peripheral to Be Used	Insert Conversational Cues
7:30–7:35	Daily Quiz (rather than spend time taking roll, students turn in a weekly sheet containing the week's daily quizzes)	Paper or transparent overhead	Document camera	Display problem (see lesson notes) to students using document camera. Solicit questions about underlying concept and equations involved.
7:35–7:40	Review of needed concepts (building on daily quiz): acceleration due to gravity, Newton's Second Law of Motion	Video	Camera one; document camera	Pose questions to random students at various sites, asking about g and $F = m \times a$.
7:40–7:55	Introduction of Atwood machine to measure g; historical perspective included	Video	Camera one; document camera	• Pose questions to random students about how to measure g using the displayed apparatus. • Progression leads to derivation of accompanying equation.

(Continued)

AP Physics—Unit Script *(Continued)*

SEGMENT	LESSON OBJECTIVE	MEDIA	EQUIPMENT	DIALOGUE
Length of Each Segment	What You Plan to Accomplish	Type of Media to Be Used	IVC Equipment/ Peripheral to Be Used	Insert Conversational Cues
7:55–8:05	Introduction of problem involving Atwood machine principles and equations	Video	Camera one	Explanation of problem and questions to determine relevancy to previously derived equation (see lesson notes).
8:05–8:10	Review of principles and equations; HW assignment	Video	Camera one; document camera	

Appendix C

Glossary

analog signals
The analog signal that is used to transmit audio and video represents variable measurable quantities (e.g., voltage) and is still used in most television, radio, and telephone lines. The codec component of the videoconference unit converts analog signals to digital signals.

application
How you make use of a technology. For example, utilizing IVC for instruction is one application of the videoconferencing technology. As you learn more about the functions of the technology itself, you'll use this knowledge and your skills to design, use, and evaluate IVC-based programs for teaching and learning. Application is also commonly used as a generic reference to computer software, particularly end-user software such as a word-processing program or spreadsheet program.

archived video stream
A stored, compressed file accessible for later reference.

asynchronous communication
Virtual learning occurs either in the form of asynchronous (not at the same time) or synchronous (immediate and face-to-face) communication between teachers and students or student to student. In the case of videoconferencing, communication occurs in a synchronous fashion. In the case of online or Internet-based instruction, interaction occurs in a manner that is asynchronous—not simultaneous and not occurring in real time. Examples of asynchronous communication include e-mail, e-mail lists, and bulletin boards.

bandwidth
Bandwidth refers to the capacity of your communications network to exchange data between two nodes on the network. Bandwidth capacity determines the amount of data—whether it is video, audio, or text—that can be transmitted through network channels in a given amount of time.

blended learning (hybrid course)
An instructional strategy incorporating a variety of delivery and participation options. A blended, or hybrid, course might offer a combination of face-to-face and virtual learning components, including interactive videoconferencing.

bridge

If you're conducting a videoconference with more than two sites participating, the bridge, also called the MCU (multipoint control unit), connects the sites so that they can all communicate at the same time.

circuit

A closed path through which electrical currents can flow; a configuration of electrically connected components or devices.

codec

Short for coder-decoder, this device is the part of your IVC system that encodes or decodes audio and video signals. It can be used to convert analog signals to digital signals and vice versa. It works much like the modem on your desktop computer. It's used in conjunction with a scan converter to convert computer video into television video. The codec can be a separate device or contained inside the same box with the scan converter.

constructivist instructional theory

A theory of learning which posits that learners construct an understanding of the world through the process of acquiring knowledge and reflecting on actual experiences. According to this theory, learning is an active and social process, not a static accumulation of data and skills.

content provider

A formal or informal educational agency that provides educational content to K–12 schools through interactive videoconferencing.

data network

An informal name for a digital network used exclusively to send data (e-mail, databases, documents, etc.) without the inclusion of video and audio. Data networks can interconnect with other networks and can contain subnetworks.

data ports

A point on your local area network (LAN) where you can plug in a device and gain access to the resources available on the network.

digital signals

Audio and video signals represented by discrete variations rather than continuously variable analog signals.

distance delivery

Instruction provided via computer or other electronic technology to learners separated by distance or time, or both.

distance education

An instructional program where the teacher and student are separated by physical space or time, or both. A variety of educational media can be employed—from workbooks or assignments (sent by mail), to web-based learning environments, to high-end, room-sized IVC systems. Some distance education programs employ synchronous teaching and learning techniques, while others employ asynchronous teaching and learning techniques.

distributed learning

Virtual learning that makes use of mixed or multimedia tools to bridge the distance between teacher and learner. Such tools include videoconferencing, online instruction, e-mail, broadcast video, telephone, Internet, and video streaming.

DS3
The data rate for this telecommunications carrier line (or T-3 line) is 44.736 Mbit/s.

early adopters
Teachers who come forward right away to experiment with emerging educational technologies and use them in their classrooms.

emerging technologies
Electronic tools and systems new to the field that have not yet been integrated or standardized.

end users
In a network situation, each participating site and its participants are end users. They are, in essence, the "customers" of the network, using the hardware and software services offered by the network.

E-rate
A program established as a result of the Telecommunications Act of 1996, E-rate provides schools and libraries discounted telecommunications and other technologies.

external devices
Also referred to as "system peripherals," these are pieces of equipment—such as VCRs, electronic whiteboards, and document cameras—that add features to an IVC system.

facilitator
The on-site individual who assists students during a videoconference and helps them learn from a virtual teacher in either a synchronous or asynchronous situation.

far-sites
Remotely located classrooms; end points of a multipoint interactive videoconference.

56K
This is the abbreviation for the highest possible data transmission rate currently available over regular phone lines. It stands for 56,000 bits per second, or 56kbps. "Switched 56K service" allows end users to dial up and transmit digital information at a rate of up to 56,000 bits per second.

gateway
This is a point on a network that serves as an entrance to another network, allowing several distributed networks to work together. Gateways are fundamental to the free-flowing of information both through the Internet and during videoconferencing.

gigabit
A unit of digital information storage. One gigabit = 10^9 = 1,000,000,000.

H.323
A video compression/communication standard, H.323 is an algorithm that ensures the interoperability of IVC units, no matter the brand name, manufacturer, or vendor. This standard was developed by a consortium of networking experts via an International Telecommunication Union study group.

hub
A device that provides a common connection point between devices on a network, where data converges from one or more directions and is then sent out again in one or more directions.

hybrid (or blended) course
A course of study composed of both traditional and virtual-learning elements.

information technology (IT) manager
The information technology manager is the person in the district who oversees all aspects of managing and processing information. IT managers are usually the go-to person for technology-related issues and the decisions that drive technology programs.

infrastructure
The sum of the physical hardware and software that makes up your videoconferencing network, allowing end users to utilize the audio and video components to communicate with people located at one or more remote sites. The hardware may include such transmission media as phone lines, cable lines, fiber optics, or satellite systems. It also includes routers, bridges, gateways, aggregators, cameras, microphones, monitors, and the software used to send and receive telecommunications signals.

interactive videoconferencing (IVC)
Two-way video and audio communication supported by a computer network or digital phone line that facilitates interaction between people in two (point-to-point) or more (multipoint) locations, creating a virtual classroom or conference room.

Internet
A worldwide network of networks, comprising telephone wires, fiber optics, satellite transmissions, and other various technologies, first developed in the 1960s by the U.S. Department of Defense. Today, the Internet connects the networks of businesses, schools, nonprofit organizations, government agencies, and so forth. There are hundreds of millions of users in hundreds of countries around the world.

Internet2
Internet2 is a not-for-profit advanced networking consortium comprising more than 200 U.S. universities in cooperation with 70 leading corporations, 45 government agencies, laboratories and other institutions of higher learning as well as over 50 international partner organizations. Internet2 members leverage a high-performance network and worldwide partnerships to support and enhance their educational and research missions.

IP address
An address on a network that identifies a particular computer or communication device. Each IP address is unique and generally has four decimal numbers. For an IP-based (Internet) videoconference, this address works like a website URL, dialing your system into the conference. For a point-to-point IVC, you can dial the other site's IP number directly, much like a phone call, avoiding use of your network's bridging services.

ISDN
ISDN stands for Integrated Services Digital Network, a digital phone line that allows the integrated transmission of voice, video, and data, facilitating global interaction via a set of protocol and interface standards.

millennials
Characterizes a cohort of the industrialized global population born roughly after 1980. They came of age in a world of rapidly emerging desktop, digital technology and tend to be exceptionally tech-savvy. Their utilization of technology applications is typically second nature. This cohort is classified in much the same way as baby boomers, a distinct and identifiable group with shared cultural and social experiences.

multipoint control unit (MCU)
MCU stands for multipoint control unit. Also frequently referred to as the "bridge," the MCU is a computerized, automated switching system that allows more than two IVC sites (or network nodes) to participate in a videoconference at the same time.

modality
A manner of teaching; a structure for sharing knowledge.

modem
A piece of hardware that allows your computer to interact with other computers across telephone lines. It converts digital signals from the Internet to analog signals that travel on phone lines.

multipoint videoconference
More than two end sites participating in an interactive videoconference. The conference must be switched through a multipoint control unit (MCU), commonly referred to as a "bridge."

peripheral
An external device such as a VCR, electronic whiteboard, or document camera that adds features and provides input to an IVC system.

picture-in-picture (PIP)
Like an inset on a map, PIP displays on the television monitor a simultaneous live broadcast of an IVC far-site (or of the home-site if you are operating with only one monitor).

point-to-point videoconference
An IVC setup that includes only two participating sites. In most cases, the connection is made using a direct-dial call that does not require the use of a hub or a multipoint control unit.

preconfigured settings
Prior to participating in an IVC class or conference, cameras and microphones should be aligned for optimal interaction during the videoconference. IVC microphones control the position of cameras during the videoconference and may be adjusted ahead of time to suit the room setup through a configuration process, often unique to different models and brands of IVC equipment. Handheld remote control units often control the tilt and zoom features of the system camera. Once the camera settings have been established, when an end user pushes the microphone button during the videoconference the camera will move to include that person in the monitor frame.

real-time access
Two-way, live, simultaneous communication; synchronous communication.

remote sites
Also referred to as "far-sites," these are the IVC participant sites that are located a distance away from your own site, or "home-site."

scan converter
Accepts data (e.g., video) from one format and converts it to another format. In videoconferencing technology, a scan converter typically converts a digital signal from a computer into an analog signal that can be displayed on a regular television monitor. Its particular role is to convert computer video scan rates (how many times per second the image is refreshed, or repainted, on the screen) to scan rates for TV video.

segment
A portion of your videoconference dedicated to a particular topic, media, or modality.

synchronous communication

Two-way interaction between teacher and learner in real time. There's no time delay in synchronous communication.

teacher of record

In a virtual learning class, this is the teacher who delivers the class and assigns the grade. The teacher may or may not be on staff in the student's home district.

telecommunications

Systems that transport information over a distance, sending and receiving audio, video and data signals through electronic means.

tent sign

A heavy piece of paper folded in half so that it will stand up, displaying student, teacher, or site name. A tent sign facilitates communication when multiple sites are involved in a videoconference.

test call

A trial call between videoconference sites prior to a scheduled IVC to ensure that the participating sites are interoperable.

T-1

This symbol represents a transmission bit rate of 1.544 million bits per second. It's equivalent to the ISDN transmission rate. In Europe, the T-1 transmission rate is 2.048 million bits per second. This term is often used as shorthand for an Internet connection that permits data transfer at this rate.

two-way interaction

In a videoconference, this means that both or all participating sites have use of audio and video communication tools; all sites can see and hear each other.

vendor

A retailer or wholesaler of products such as educational technology hardware and software.

video network

Same as a data network, only dedicated exclusively to video. Often employed to ensure high quality video and to protect the integrity of the data network. (See "data network.")

video streaming

Delivery of a compressed video file over an IP connection such as the Internet or an Intranet. The streaming process allows end users to view the file without first downloading it onto their own computer. The video is stored only temporarily on the viewer's computer (although users can also save the file onto their hard drive if they wish).

virtual classroom

An electronic classroom consisting of off-site students (who could be in several locations), where instruction involves the synchronous or asynchronous use of electronic learning tools such as videoconferencing, online classrooms, whiteboards, chat rooms, document cameras, and so forth.

virtual course delivery

A method of course delivery via web-based instruction, online sources, CDs, videos, and/or videoconferencing. The delivery of the course content takes place from a distance, and the teacher is separated from the students by space or time, or both.

virtual field trip
A simulated, real-time field trip. In the case of videoconferencing, students interact, in a live event, with a remotely located field trip host.

virtual learning
Employing information and communication technologies to deliver instruction. Virtual learning is a term frequently used interchangeably with distance learning, online learning, e-learning, or web-based learning.

virtual learning environments
A learning environment where teacher and student are separated by time or space, or both, and the teacher provides course content through course management applications, multimedia resources, the Internet, videoconferencing, and so forth. Students receive the content and communicate with the teachers through the same technologies.

virtual student
A learner who, through electronic means, accesses courseware and instruction, learns concepts and content, asks questions of a remote teacher, and sends the remote teacher work for assessment purposes.

virtual teacher
An instructor who, through electronic means, provides courseware and instruction, responds to students' questions, and provides feedback and course assessment.

webcasting
A transmission of sound and images via the World Wide Web.

WebCT
The commercial name for a learning management system that provides interactive instructional tools for an online proprietary virtual learning environment.

World Wide Web
A smaller network within Internet1, the World Wide Web is a portion of the Internet comprised of a constellation of networked resources. Its Internet servers utilize HTTP to transfer documents and multimedia files formatted in hypertext markup language (HTML). Not all servers on the Internet are part of the World Wide Web.

Appendix D

References
and Resources

References

Alberta Education. (2006). *Video-conferencing research community of practice: Research report.* Retrieved December 2, 2008, from http://education.alberta.ca/media/822749/vccopreport.pdf

Amirian, S. (2003, October). *Pedagogy & videoconferencing: A review of recent literature.* A poster session presentation at NJEDge.NET Conference, Plainsboro, NJ.

Anderson, T. (2008). Is videoconferencing the killer app for K–12 distance education? *Journal of Distance Education, 22*(2), 109–124.

Andrews, T., Smyth, R., Tynan, B., Vale, D., & Caladine, R. (2008). Rich media technologies and uncertain futures: Developing sustainable, scalable models. In *Hello! Where are you in the landscape of educational technology? Proceedings ascilite Melbourne 2008.* www.ascilite.org.au/conferences/melbourne08/procs/andrews.pdf

AYA/ELA (2004). *Candidate guide to national board certification.* Retrieved January 5, 2004, from www.nbpts.org/candidates/guide/04port/04_ayaela_instructions/04_aya_ela_resources.pdf

Berge, Z. L., & Mrozowski, S. (2001). Review of research in distance education 1990–1999 [Special issue]. *American Journal of Distance Education, 15*(3), 5–19.

Bershin, J. (2004). *The blended book of learning.* San Francisco: Pfeiffer.

Branzburg, J. (2001). Videoconferencing? *Technology & Learning, 22*(2), 54–57.

Crews, K. (2003, April 8). *New copyright law for distance education: The meaning and importance of the TEACH Act.* Article prepared for the American Library Association. Chicago: American Library Association.

Davis, N. E., & Niederhauser, D. S. (2007). Virtual schooling. *Learning & Leading with Technology, 34*(7), 10–15

Dede, C. (1996). Emerging technologies and distributed learning. *The American Journal of Distance Education, 10*(2), 4–36.

Digital Millennium Copyright Act of 1998. (1998). Pub. L. No. 105-304, 112 Stat. 2860.

Dyck, B. (2008). *Using technology to bridge understanding for foreign- and second-language learners.* Retrieved December 2, 2008, from www.education-world.com/a_tech/columnists/dyck/dyck027.shtml

Foshee, D. (1997). *Planning the smart classroom: A practical primer for designing interactive video learning environments.* Austin, TX: VTel Corp.

Goldberg, L. (2002, March 20). Our technology future. *Education Week, 21*(27), 32, 34. Retrieved November 13, 2003, from www.edweek.org/ew/newstory.cfm?slug=27goldberg.h21

Greenberg, A. (2004, February). *Videoconferencing-based distance education: A platform for understanding research into the technology's effectiveness and value.* Pleasanton, CA: Wainhouse Research. Retrieved November 6, 2002, from http://research.newarchitectmag.com

Greenberg, A., & Colbert, R. (2002, October). *Best practices in live content acquisition by distance learning organizations: Enhancing the primary and secondary school classroom by tapping content resources via two-way interactive video.* Pleasanton, CA: Wainhouse Research. Retrieved November 6, 2002, from http://research.newarchitectmag.com

Hanor, J., & Hayden, K. (2003). *Improving learning for all students through technology (ILAST).* [Abstract]. Retrieved November 10, 2003, from www.ilast.org

Heath, M. J. (1997). *The design, development, and implementation of a virtual online classroom.* Unpublished doctoral dissertation. University of Houston, Texas.

Holznagel, D. D. (2003). *Access and opportunity: Policy options for interactive video in K–12 education.* Portland, OR: Northwest Regional Educational Laboratory.

Kober, N. (1990). Think rural means isolated? Not when distance learning reaches into school. *The School Administrator, 47*(10), 16–24.

Learning Circuits. (2006). *Learning circuits: 2006 Survey of learning management dystems.* Retrieved on December 12, 2006, from www.learningcircuits.org/2006/August/2006LMSresults.htm

Martin, M. (2005). Seeing is believing: The role of videoconferencing in distance learning. *British Journal of Educational Technology, 36*(3), 397–405.

McAnear, A. (2007, February). What does globalization mean for education? *Learning & Leading with Technology, 34*(5), 5.

McKenzie, J. (2003). Pedagogy does matter. *The Ed Tech Journal, 13*(1.1), 2. Retrieved December 16, 2003, from www.fno.org/sept03/pedagogy.html

McMahan, K. (1998, August). Effective communication and information sharing in virtual teams. In Regis University (Ed.) *WWW482M teams: Theory and practice* (Report No. 200019, pp. 1–12). Denver, CO: Regis University, Department of Business Administration.

Mendenhall, R. (2007, January). Challenging the myths about distance learning. *Distance Learning Today, 1*(1), 4–5.

Moore, M. G. (1991). *Theory of distance education* [Monograph]. University Park, PA: American Center for the Study of Distance Education.

No Child Left Behind Act of 2001. (2002). Pub. L. No. 107-110, 115 Stat. 1426.

Pachnowski, L. (2002). Virtual field trips through videoconferencing. *Learning and Leading with Technology, 29*(6), 12.

Perraton, H., Creed, C., & Robinson, B. (2002). Teacher education guidelines: Using open and distance learning. Technology, curriculum, cost, evaluation (Report No. SP 041 013). Paris, France: UNESCO Higher Education Division. (ERIC Document Reproduction Service No. ED468705.

Sullivan, M., Jolly, D., Foster, D., & Tompkins, R. (1994). *Local heroes: A guidebook for bringing telecommunications to rural, small schools.* Austin, TX: Southwest Educational Development Laboratory.

Technology, Education, and Copyright Harmonization (TEACH) Act of 2001. (2002). Pub. L. No. 107–273, 116 Stat. 1758.

U.S. Department of Education. (2003). *Tear down those walls: The revolution is underway.* Available from www.ed.gov/about/offices/list/os/technology/plan/2004/site/theplan/edlite-TearDownThoseWalls.html

U.S. Department of Education, National Center for Educational Statistics. (2001). Cattagni, A., & Farris, E. *Internet access in U. S. public schools: 1994–2000.* (NCES 2001-071). Washington, DC: U. S. Government Printing Office.

Vincent, J. (2003). Individual difference, technology and the teacher of the future. *Australian Computer Society, Inc.* Melbourne, Australia: IFIP Working Groups 3.1 and 3.3 Working Group Conference.

Ward Melville Heritage Organization. (2002, March). Videoconferencing exposes students to new worlds. *T.H.E. Journal Online.* Retrieved June 7, 2002, from www.thejournal.com/magazine/vault/A3945C.fm?kw=719

Willis, J. (2007). Cooperative learning is a brain turn on. *Middle School Journal, 38*(4), 4–13.

Zohoori, A. R. (1997). *Teaching on television from concept to evaluation.* In Competition-Connection-Collaboration. Proceedings of the Annual Conference on Distance Teaching and Learning (13th, Madison, Wisconsin, August 6–8, 1997). (ERIC Document Reproduction Service no. 413 870)

Resources

Aleksic-Maslac, K., & Jeren, B. (2001, August). Asynchronous distance learning model. *International conference on engineering education* (pp. 13–16). Oslo, Norway: International Conference on Engineering Education.

Bigham, S., Kellogg, J., & Hodges, J. (Eds.). (n.d.) *Telecommunications technology planning manual.* Nashville, TN: South Central Bell.

Blank, M. (1999). Everything you ever wanted to know about H.323. *Teleconferencing Magazine.* Retrieved October 25, 2003, from www.teleconferencemagazine.com

Budniewski, D. (2003, October 23). DEVO take UB classroom to the global community. *University at Buffalo Reporter, 35*(9). Retrieved April 16, 2004, from http://people.uis.edu/rschr1/onlinelearning/archive/2003_10_19_archive.html

Cashman, S. (2003). *Discovering computers: A gateway to information.* Boston: Course Technology.

Cavanaugh, C. S. (2001). The effectiveness of interactive distance education technologies in K–12 learning: A meta-analysis. *International Journal of Educational Telecommunications, 7*(1), 73–88.

Clark, T. (2001). *Virtual schools: Trends and issues. A study of virtual schools in the United States.* Phoenix, AZ: Distance Learning Resource Network at WestEd. Retrieved October 18, 2002, from www.wested.org/online_pubs/virtualschools.pdf

Curtis, D. (2007). Choose the right technology. *Interactive Educator, 3*(2), 22–27.

deFord, K., & Dimock, V. (2002, June). Understanding the value of interactive videoconferencing technology in improving K–12 educational systems: Vol. 1. *Interactive videoconferencing: A policy issues review,* 1–7. A Regional Technology in Education Consortia National Collaborative Project. Washington, DC: Regional Technology in Education Consortia.

Donnell-Kay Foundation (2007). *Trujillo Commission on online education: Final findings and recommendations.* Denver, CO: Author.

EdLiNC and NCTET. (2007). *E-rate: 10 years of connecting kids and community.* Washington DC: Education and Libraries Networks Coalition. Available at www.edlinc.org/pdf/NCTETReport_212.pdf

Green, K. (2003, December). Tracking the digital puck into 2004. *Syllabus Magazine.* Retrieved November 13, 2003, from www.syllabus.com/article.asp?id=8574

Hanson, D., Maushak, N., Scholosser, C., Anderson, M., Sorensen, C., & Simonson, M. (1997). *Distance education: Review of the literature.* Bloomington, Indiana: Association for Educational Communications & Technology.

Hayden, K. (1999). Videoconferencing in K–12 Education: A Delphi study of characteristics and critical strategies to support constructivist learning experiences. (Doctoral dissertation, Pepperdine University, 1999). *Dissertation Abstract International, 60, 06A.*

Heath, M., & Holznagel, D. (2002, June). Understanding the value of interactive video-conferencing technology. *Interactive videoconferencing: A literature review. Vol. 1.* A Regional Technology in Education Consortia National Collaborative Project. Washington, DC: Regional Technology in Education Consortia.

Holznagel, D. C. (2003, June). *Access and opportunity: Policy options for interactive video in K–12 education.* Symposium conducted at the meeting of the Regional Educational Laboratory and Educational Technology Consortium Practitioners, Dallas, Texas.

Hopkins, G. L. (1995). *The ISDN literacy book.* New York: Addison-Wesley.

Interactive videoconferencing in K–12 settings. (2002, October). Regional Technology in Education Consortia paper presented at A Symposium for Practitioners, Dallas, Texas.

Johnstone, S. M., & Witherspoon, J. P. (2001, March). *Quality in online education: Results from a revolution [Special issue], 15*(3). Retrieved on May 12, 2002, from www.usdla.org/ED_magazine/illuminactive/MAR01_Issue/index.html

Kerca, S. (1996). *Distance learning, the Internet, and the World Wide Web.* East Lansing, MI: National Center for Research on Teacher Learning. (ERIC Document Reproduction Service No. ED395214

Kiciman, E., & Fox, A. (2001, May). *A separation of concerns in networks service composition.* Paper presented at International Conference on Software Engineering (ICSE), Toronto, Canada.

Kozma, R. B. (Ed.). (2003). *Technology, innovation, and educational change: A global perspective.* Eugene, OR: International Society for Educational Technology.

Krell, E. Videoconferencing gets the call. *Training.* Retrieved August 2, 2002, from Proquest: www.vanderbilt.edu/library

Kuralt, C. (1990). *A life on the road.* New York: G. P. Putnam's Sons.

Kvaternik, R. (2002). *Teacher education guidelines: Using open and distance learning.* Paris: UNESCO.

Lockett, E., & Strode-Penny, L. (1998, September 24, 25). *Child studies educational videoconferencing.* Paper presented at Learning Technologies '98, Queensland, Australia.

McMahan, K. (1998). *Distance educator's desk guide* (Business Administration Capstone), Regis University, Denver, CO. Abstract retrieved September 13, 2003, from www.bizresources.com/learning/de deskguide.html

Merrick, S. (2007). *Innovate Online Articles.* Retrieved January 4, 2007, from Innovate Online: www.innovateonline.info/index.php?view=article&id=24

Mitchell, J. (1997, March). *Educational videoconferencing: Critical success factors.* Paper presented at the Delivering Flexible Learning in Training and Education conference, Sidney, Australia.

Moore, M. G. (1993). Theory of transactional distance. In D. Keegan (Ed.), *Theoretical principles of distance education* (pp. 22–37). London, New York: Routledge.

Moore, M. G., & Kearsley, G. (1996). *Distance education: A systems view.* Boston: Wadsworth.

Muilenburg, L., S. & Berge, Z. (2001). Barriers of distance education: A factor analytic study. *The American Journal of Distance Education, 15*(2), 7-24.

Mullane, J., & Cataline, J. (2002, Spring). Harness the power of videoconferencing through ongoing support. *FETC Connections, 1,* 6-7.

National Research Council. (2002). J. D. Bransford, A. L. Brown, & R. R. Cocking (Eds.), *How people learn: Brain, mind, experience and school* (Expanded edition). Washington, DC: National Academy Press.

Negroponte, N., Resnick, M., & Cassell, J. (n.d.). *Creating a learning revolution.* Abstract retrieved August 29, 2002, from www.unesco.org/education/educprog/lwf/doc/protfolio/opinion8.htm

North Central Regional Educational Laboratory. (2003). *Indicator: Technology-ready facilities.* Abstract retrieved October 9, 2003, from www.ncrel.org/engauge/framewk/acc/facility/accfacra.htm

Northwest Educational Technology Consortium and Northwest Regional Educational Laboratory. (2000). Issues for K–12 decision makers. *Digital bridges: Videoconferencing for teaching and learning.* Portland, OR: Northwest Educational Technology Consortium.

Northwest Educational Technology Consortium and Northwest Regional Educational Laboratory. (2000). Promising practices for K–12 videoconferencing. *Digital bridges: Videoconferencing for teaching and learning.* Portland, OR: Northwest Education Technology Consortium.

Ray, K. (2002). *A history of videoconferencing.* Unpublished manuscript. Nashville, TN: Vanderbilt University.

Ray, K. (2002, September). *Increasing science literacy through virtual connections* [Short paper/poster]. Presented at Conference on Ontological, Epistemological, Linguistic and Pedagogical Considerations of Language and Science Literacy: Empowering Research and Informing Instruction, Victoria, British Columbia, Canada.

Saba, F. (2003). *Distance education: A systems approach.* PDF file available from Distance Educator.com.

SETDA. (2007). *SETDA's National Trends Report 2007.* Washington DC: State Education Technology Director's Association. Available at www.setda.org/web/guest/2007NationalTrendsReport

Shearer, R. L. (2003). Interaction in distance education. *Distance Educator Special Report 2*(1). Madison, WI: Atwood Publishing.

Sherry, L. (1996). Issues in distance learning. *International Journal of Educational Telecommunications, 1*(4), 337-365.

Sherry, L., & Morse, R. (1995). An assessment of training needs in the use of distance education for instruction. *International Journal of Educational Telecommunications, 1*(1), 5-22. Reprinted (1996, Winter) in *Educational Technology Review, 5,* 10-17.

Specialist Schools Trust. (2000, July). *One world one school.* Paper presented at Vision 2020 Conference, Dartford, United Kingdom. Retrieved January 11, 2004, from www.schoolsnetwork.org.uk

Spellings, M. (2005). *No child left behind: Expanding the promise.* Washington DC: Education Publications Center, U.S. Department of Education.

SREB. (2004). *Using rigor, relevance, and relationships to improve student achievement.* Atlanta, GA: Southern Regional Education Board.

Tapscott, D. (1998). *Growing up digital.* New York: McGraw Hill.

Tapscott, D. (1998). *The net generation and the school.* Retrieved November 10, 2000, from the Milken Exchange on Education Technology website: www.mff.org

Technology, Education, and Copyright Harmonization (TEACH) Act of 2001. (2002). Pub. L. No. 107-273, 116 Stat. 1758.

Ullman, E. (2007). Future proofing students: Preparing students to succeed in the global workforce. *Interactive Educator, 3*(3), 23–27.

UNESCO. (1997). *World communications report: The media and the challenges of the new technologies.* Paris: Author.

UNESCO. (1998a). *World education report 1998: Teachers and teaching in a changing world* (Summary), Paris: Author. Available online: www.unesco.org/education/educprog/ wer/wer.htm

UNESCO. (1998b). *Creating learning networks for African teachers.* Available online: www.unesco.org/education /unesco/educprog/lwf/doc/IA1.html

UNESCO Education News. (1998, September/November). Ambitious plan for teachers. *Copy Editor, 14,* 1–2. Available online: www.unesco.org/education/educnews/sept/cd14.pdf.

U.S. Department of Education, National Center for Education Statistics. (2002). *A profile of participation in distance education, 1999–2000,* by Anna C. Sikora. (NCES 2003–154). Washington, DC: U. S. Government Printing Office.

Weigel, V. B. (2002). *Deep learning for a digital age: Technology's untapped potential to enrich higher education.* New York: Jossey-Bass.

National Educational Technology Standards

National Educational Technology Standards for Students (NETS•S)

All K–12 students should be prepared to meet the following standards and performance indicators.

1. **Creativity and Innovation**

   Students demonstrate creative thinking, construct knowledge, and develop innovative products and processes using technology. Students:

   a. apply existing knowledge to generate new ideas, products, or processes

   b. create original works as a means of personal or group expression

   c. use models and simulations to explore complex systems and issues

   d. identify trends and forecast possibilities

2. **Communication and Collaboration**

   Students use digital media and environments to communicate and work collaboratively, including at a distance, to support individual learning and contribute to the learning of others. Students:

   a. interact, collaborate, and publish with peers, experts, or others employing a variety of digital environments and media

   b. communicate information and ideas effectively to multiple audiences using a variety of media and formats

   c. develop cultural understanding and global awareness by engaging with learners of other cultures

   d. contribute to project teams to produce original works or solve problems

3. **Research and Information Fluency**

   Students apply digital tools to gather, evaluate, and use information. Students:

   a. plan strategies to guide inquiry

   b. locate, organize, analyze, evaluate, synthesize, and ethically use information from a variety of sources and media

   c. evaluate and select information sources and digital tools based on the appropriateness to specific tasks

   d. process data and report results

4. **Critical Thinking, Problem Solving, and Decision Making**

   Students use critical-thinking skills to plan and conduct research, manage projects, solve problems, and make informed decisions using appropriate digital tools and resources. Students:

   a. identify and define authentic problems and significant questions for investigation

   b. plan and manage activities to develop a solution or complete a project

   c. collect and analyze data to identify solutions and make informed decisions

   d. use multiple processes and diverse perspectives to explore alternative solutions

5. **Digital Citizenship**

   Students understand human, cultural, and societal issues related to technology and practice legal and ethical behavior. Students:

   a. advocate and practice the safe, legal, and responsible use of information and technology

   b. exhibit a positive attitude toward using technology that supports collaboration, learning, and productivity

   c. demonstrate personal responsibility for lifelong learning

   d. exhibit leadership for digital citizenship

6. **Technology Operations and Concepts**

   Students demonstrate a sound understanding of technology concepts, systems, and operations. Students:

   a. understand and use technology systems

   b. select and use applications effectively and productively

   c. troubleshoot systems and applications

   d. transfer current knowledge to the learning of new technologies

National Educational Technology Standards for Teachers (NETS•T)

All classroom teachers should be prepared to meet the following standards and performance indicators.

1. **Facilitate and Inspire Student Learning and Creativity**

    Teachers use their knowledge of subject matter, teaching and learning, and technology to facilitate experiences that advance student learning, creativity, and innovation in both face-to-face and virtual environments. Teachers:

    a. promote, support, and model creative and innovative thinking and inventiveness

    b. engage students in exploring real-world issues and solving authentic problems using digital tools and resources

    c. promote student reflection using collaborative tools to reveal and clarify students' conceptual understanding and thinking, planning, and creative processes

    d. model collaborative knowledge construction by engaging in learning with students, colleagues, and others in face-to-face and virtual environments

2. **Design and Develop Digital-Age Learning Experiences and Assessments**

    Teachers design, develop, and evaluate authentic learning experiences and assessments incorporating contemporary tools and resources to maximize content learning in context and to develop the knowledge, skills, and attitudes identified in the NETS•S. Teachers:

    a. design or adapt relevant learning experiences that incorporate digital tools and resources to promote student learning and creativity

    b. develop technology-enriched learning environments that enable all students to pursue their individual curiosities and become active participants in setting their own educational goals, managing their own learning, and assessing their own progress

    c. customize and personalize learning activities to address students' diverse learning styles, working strategies, and abilities using digital tools and resources

    d. provide students with multiple and varied formative and summative assessments aligned with content and technology standards and use resulting data to inform learning and teaching

3. Model Digital-Age Work and Learning

Teachers exhibit knowledge, skills, and work processes representative of an innovative professional in a global and digital society. Teachers:

a. demonstrate fluency in technology systems and the transfer of current knowledge to new technologies and situations

b. collaborate with students, peers, parents, and community members using digital tools and resources to support student success and innovation

c. communicate relevant information and ideas effectively to students, parents, and peers using a variety of digital-age media and formats

d. model and facilitate effective use of current and emerging digital tools to locate, analyze, evaluate, and use information resources to support research and learning

4. Promote and Model Digital Citizenship and Responsibility

Teachers understand local and global societal issues and responsibilities in an evolving digital culture and exhibit legal and ethical behavior in their professional practices. Teachers:

a. advocate, model, and teach safe, legal, and ethical use of digital information and technology, including respect for copyright, intellectual property, and the appropriate documentation of sources

b. address the diverse needs of all learners by using learner-centered strategies and providing equitable access to appropriate digital tools and resources

c. promote and model digital etiquette and responsible social interactions related to the use of technology and information

d. develop and model cultural understanding and global awareness by engaging with colleagues and students of other cultures using digital-age communication and collaboration tools

5. Engage in Professional Growth and Leadership

Teachers continuously improve their professional practice, model lifelong learning, and exhibit leadership in their school and professional community by promoting and demonstrating the effective use of digital tools and resources. Teachers:

a. participate in local and global learning communities to explore creative applications of technology to improve student learning

b. exhibit leadership by demonstrating a vision of technology infusion, participating in shared decision making and community building, and developing the leadership and technology skills of others

c. evaluate and reflect on current research and professional practice on a regular basis to make effective use of existing and emerging digital tools and resources in support of student learning

d. contribute to the effectiveness, vitality, and self-renewal of the teaching profession and of their school and community

National Educational Technology Standards for Administrators (NETS•A)

All school administrators should be prepared to meet the following standards and performance indicators.

I. Leadership and Vision

Educational leaders inspire a shared vision for comprehensive integration of technology and foster an environment and culture conducive to the realization of that vision. Educational leaders:

    A. facilitate the shared development by all stakeholders of a vision for technology use and widely communicate that vision.

    B. maintain an inclusive and cohesive process to develop, implement, and monitor
a dynamic, long-range, and systemic technology plan to achieve the vision.

    C. foster and nurture a culture of responsible risk taking and advocate policies promoting continuous innovation with technology.

    D. use data in making leadership decisions.

    E. advocate research-based effective practices in use of technology.

    F. advocate, on the state and national levels, policies, programs, and funding opportunities that support implementation of the district technology plan.

II. Learning and Teaching

Educational leaders ensure that curricular design, instructional strategies, and learning environments integrate appropriate technologies to maximize learning and teaching. Educational leaders:

    A. identify, use, evaluate, and promote appropriate technologies to enhance and support instruction and standards-based curriculum leading to high levels of student achievement.

    B. facilitate and support collaborative technology-enriched learning environments conducive to innovation for improved learning.

    C. provide for learner-centered environments that use technology to meet the individual and diverse needs of learners.

    D. facilitate the use of technologies to support and enhance instructional methods that develop higher-level thinking, decision-making, and problem-solving skills.

    E. provide for and ensure that faculty and staff take advantage of quality professional learning opportunities for improved learning and teaching with technology.

III. Productivity and Professional Practice

Educational leaders apply technology to enhance their professional practice and to increase their own productivity and that of others. Educational leaders:

    A. model the routine, intentional, and effective use of technology.

    B. employ technology for communication and collaboration among colleagues, staff, parents, students, and the larger community.

    C. create and participate in learning communities that stimulate, nurture, and support faculty and staff in using technology for improved productivity.

    D. engage in sustained, job-related professional learning using technology resources.

    E. maintain awareness of emerging technologies and their potential uses in education.

    F. use technology to advance organizational improvement.

IV. Support, Management, and Operations

Educational leaders ensure the integration of technology to support productive systems for learning and administration. Educational leaders:

    A. develop, implement, and monitor policies and guidelines to ensure compatibility of technologies.

    B. implement and use integrated technology-based management and operations systems.

    C. allocate financial and human resources to ensure complete and sustained implementation of the technology plan.

    D. integrate strategic plans, technology plans, and other improvement plans and policies to align efforts and leverage resources.

    E. implement procedures to drive continuous improvements of technology systems and to support technology-replacement cycles.

V. Assessment and Evaluation

Educational leaders use technology to plan and implement comprehensive systems of effective assessment and evaluation. Educational leaders:

    A. use multiple methods to assess and evaluate appropriate uses of technology resources for learning, communication, and productivity.

    B. use technology to collect and analyze data, interpret results, and communicate findings to improve instructional practice and student learning.

    C. assess staff knowledge, skills, and performance in using technology and use results to facilitate quality professional development and to inform personnel decisions.

    D. use technology to assess, evaluate, and manage administrative and operational systems.

VI. Social, Legal, and Ethical Issues

Educational leaders understand the social, legal, and ethical issues related to technology and model responsible decision making related to these issues. Educational leaders:

- **A.** ensure equity of access to technology resources that enable and empower all learners and educators.

- **B.** identify, communicate, model, and enforce social, legal, and ethical practices to promote responsible use of technology.

- **C.** promote and enforce privacy, security, and online safety related to the use of technology.

- **D.** promote and enforce environmentally safe and healthy practices in the use of technology.

- **E.** participate in the development of policies that clearly enforce copyright law and assign ownership of intellectual property developed with district resources.